THE

BIBLE

SUMMARY

for

REAL PEOPLE

DR. SHAWN GREENER

To order additional copies of this book, contact:
Bookwhip
1-855-339-3589
https://www.bookwhip.com

This is an unapologetic, real world, real people Entire Bible Commentary. So what? Who cares what a potential Bible nerd has to say. Well, in addition to living life a good bit before I took on the vest and pocket protector of Bible nerds, I experienced an awful lot, good and bad that life has to offer. Now, as I approach the last segment of my life, I thought you might benefit from a little bit of what I learned so far and this close to the end.

People often assume that a guy with a master's and doctorate degree in Theology is a stuffy and religious nerd. The truth is, I am just a regular dude and I tend to reject ultra academic religious rhetoric, Christian buzzwords and phrases. I know religious theological discourse has its place, but I tend to believe that real heady *Christianese* should only be in academia… and for me, **only** in academia.

My personal policy is to no longer attend *"pastor's conferences"* unless I am the keynote speaker. I know, seems pretty arrogant, and nothing against other pastors, but there is a reason and here it is… Like it or not.

Part of the reason is an alarming and growing percentage of the pastors (not all) spend part of their time bemoaning their pay, congregations, bemoaning the job of pastor, whining about how *"broken"* they are and yet while spending their time still measuring each other with the world's measurements.

While we are at it, can somebody tell me why so much of modern worship music and postmodern emergent western evangelical pastors are constantly talking about how *"broken"* they are? It seems like the new thing to repeatedly repeat redundantly over and over… again and again, just how "broken they are."

I am not so sure, but I think it might be the skinny jeans they all seem to be wearing these days. I could be jealous though, I am not skinny enough to wear skinny jeans, more like, husky jeans.

Lest you think I am insensitive to the struggles of pastors and their families, when I so frequently hear the laments of pastors, young and even a few old, of their chosen career or calling, I have to ask, what changed in pastoring over the past several decades?

The questions these pastors at the normal pastors conferences ask each other:

> *"What is your attendance running?"*
> *"What is your budget looking like?"*
> *"How many services are you running every Sunday?"*
> *"Do you have a yearly sabbatical?"*
> *"What is your benefits package?"*
> *"What is your salary package?"*
> *"How is your band?"*

Come to think of it, when I hear some of these Gawdly 'Right Reverend' men, and some women pray, it sounds as though they just departed Westminster Abbey after being schooled at Oxford Theological Seminary from kindergarten to post graduate!

I often could swear I could hear a regal British accent when they are praying and preaching... You talk with them once they are off the stage and the spotlight is off of them and their deep in the holler Kentucky accent returns...

No offense to Kentucky, I love Kentuckians and their accents, but you get what I mean... What I don't like is the fake regal ultra Theologian accents, unless of course they are FROM there.... To be clearer, I simply don't like fake, self-impressed people, especially in the pulpit. I bring this delicate subject up because I believe many pastors need to toughen up.

I wrote my first book, <u>*Excellence Killed the Church, How Mediocrity is Destroying America*</u> because after taking a three-year examination of "the church" in America, I deduced that we were in real trouble.

Why? Fraud. Fake. Show Church. **Show Pastors**. I am concurrently finishing a book after this one you hold, entitled *"#FraudLife"* which deeply and very frankly examines socially acceptable micro lies and macro lies. This is one of the reasons I wrote The Bible Summary for REAL People. Truth, simple Truth available to all.

Lying is also killing us, but so too is embellishing things which do not require embellishment. The Holy Bible is one such thing. The Holy Scripture needs no embellishment or fluffing up. We are warned against adding or taking away from God's Word to man.

It is very true that it is vitally important to understand the context of each passage...

Who was the author?
Where was he/she from?
What was their culture?
What was the culture and context to which that passage is written?

All of that matters greatly. Little things don't mean a lot. No, little things mean everything!

This "REAL" Bible Summary and Commentary was written so that it is very simple to read and it is my personal assessment of the Books of the Bible in about two hundred and fifty words... the "meat of it" so to speak.

What it wasn't and isn't intended to be, is apastoral or academic commentary.

This is MY commentary. These are MY impressions of the Sacred Books and what they came to mean to **me.**

These books might impact you differently; however, this is how these precious and inspired words, over the years, have moved and more importantly, **changed** me.

I am not constrained in this summary/commentary to academic and theological convention so you will experience my true and unfiltered reactions to the Books of the Bible. You will experience my real and raw emotions. Remember to pay close attention to the format of the introduction of the Books... especially "To Whom Written" or as I would more plainly put it, "the audience."

The **audience** matters.
The **context** matters.

Please know and understand that what follows is by no means an exhaustive reference, rather as I read through the Holy Scriptures this, the 34th, and most likely, last time in my life, these are the things that jump out at me... These are the things that pursue ME... As you begin this reading of my *The Bible Summary for REAL People*, KEEP pursuing after God... The teachings of Jesus, Yeshua Hamashiach, learn and do them... Never ever stop. When you fall down or fail... Dust yourself off and stand again.

I want to express my very deepest appreciation for Master's International School of Divinity and its amazing Professors for pressing me throughout their prerequisite Bible Mastery Course. If you are an adult learner seeking Spiritual growth and maturity as you may have experienced, you can do no better than my Alma Mater, www.Mdivs.edu

THE OLD TESTAMENT

Some in modernity believe The Old Testament is no longer relevant for study outside of seminary and divinity school. I vigorously disagree. The connections between the old and new testaments is inextricably linked. In fact, you simply cannot fully understand the New Testament without having a full understand of the Old Testament... It is like fuel without a car! One's understanding of the Power of the New Testament begins, is solidified and set in the Old Testament because one cannot fully understand the strength of this statement....

It is absolutely critical that you grasp this powerful and often missed fact that the Old Testament is NOT simply an irrelevant part one of a two part series. No, The Old Testament is indeed the What to the Why.... And Yeshua, Jesus Christ of Nazareth, Victor of death and our sin, my friend, I tell you this without restraint or hesitation...

Yeshua Hamashiach, Jesus Christ, He is the How.

Book of the Bible – Genesis or *"Bereshith"*
Author - Moses
Date of Writing – Details from Creation Story to the story of the death of Joseph – 19th Century B.C.
Number of Chapters - 50
To Whom Written – All of Mankind
Purpose of the Writing – To answer the pivotal question; "How did it all begin?"

My Personal Summary–

Genesis is Hebrew for "origin" or "generation" or "beginnings." Bereshith = (Hebrew word for Genesis.) Even the title of this book speaks of beginnings of many things; mankind, sin, death, and God's unwavering Hand in our redemption.

It is interesting to note that the very beginnings of this terrafirma were made in and by Perfection. Man was made by a Perfect God, in what could confidently be called, a perfect place. Yet, sin began shortly thereafter.

Genesis 6:9 – 9:17 detail the seemingly incongruous order for Noah, a man who never built a boat, to build an Ark, for rain that had never been seen on earth, and a never before seen flood, and Noah's unwavering obedient response. At all cost.

Genesis gets quickly to the point in addressing the questions that circle about even the most moderate of minds:

"How did the earth begin?"
Genesis answers, God spoke it so.

"How did man get here?"
Genesis answers, God spoke it so.

I must conclude then that God has also a perfectly ordered plan for all of mankind despite our fallen state stemming from our departure from His perfect order.

Genesis speaks to the questions of God's Holiness, righteousness, mercy and grace. God does not shield us from the lesson of sin and its consequences; rather He shows us our beginnings, failings, and foibles to point us to His Son Yeshua… The Redemption King!

We have the opportunity to re-do our lives excerpting the sin of our Fathers. Genesis is a book of choices, so is life.

Do you want to hear Rev. Dr. Shawn preach this and others in hilarious, riveting and powerful sermons to a LIVE audience?

For Desktop and to download our FREE Android and iPhone Apps https://www.spreaker.com/show/the-ninja-pastor-radio-show

Book of the Bible – Exodus Greek word – "Ek" mean "out" and "Hodos" meaning "road." In other words, *"The Road Out."*
Author - Moses
Date of Writing – Birth of Moses – Construction of the Temple 1525 – 1446 B.C.
Number of Chapters - 40
To Whom Written – All of mankind, specifically the Israelites.
Purpose of the Writing – To detail the birth pains of a nation so that travails of birth would never be forgotten.

My Personal Summary–

The beginnings of a nation are surely difficult with many obstacles to best and hurdles to clear. It was no different in the case of God's Chosen people, Israel. This with one exception; Israel is a nation chosen by God Himself. God birthed this nation. God disciplined this nation. God raised this nation.

The nation of Israel began with a family of only 70 people yet today Israel, though a tiny nation measured in square miles is great in historical stature. The Book of Exodus details the reluctant leadership of the "rags to royalty to rags" humility of Moses. Exodus begins the account of the oppression of Israel by Egypt.

Following thereafter is the childhood of Moses life. Exodus; it can be reasoned, is a revelation of the calling of Moses by God Himself to demand the freedom of God's people from Pharaohs rule. The forty-year journey through the wilderness ended up being a series of lessons taught by God to the wandering Israelites. The Book of Exodus concludes with the establishment of Hebrew culture and Law given by God.

Exodus feels much like an account of a high level of divine education at a tremendous cost. This cost would pale in comparison to the cost Yeshua Hamashiach the long awaited Messiah would pay for my sins, redemption. Neither my redemption, nor the Hebrew people's redemption would come cheaply. Ultimately we need to fear God more than we fear anything else and God will do mighty things through our obedience.

I want to briefly discuss a mistranslation of one of the Ten Commandments... It is a huge issue but few really want to address it... You've heard, "Do not take the Lord's Name in vain."

From Exodus 20:7, the Third Commandment reads: *You shall not take the name of the LORD your God in vain, for the LORD will not hold him guiltless who takes his name in vain.*

So, what does this mean? Literally, this means to falsify who God is and what He stands for.

In the original Biblical Hebrew, literally, *do not CARRY the Lord's Name in vain.*

#3

"You shall not (*lo'*) lift up, bear, or advance (*nasa'* – support or desire, forgive or dignify, respect or tolerate / you shall not deceive or delude, deploy clever tricks, beguiling people, causing them to miss the Way) through (*'eth* – with) the name or reputation (*shem*) of Yahowah, your God (efei *'elohym*), accordingly (*la* – with the intent to promote or effect), lifeless and worthless deception or devastating and destructive falsehood (*shav'* / *show'* – lies which nullify our existence leading to emptiness and nothingness, vain promises which are deceitful, desolate, ineffectual, futile, and ruinous), for indeed (*ky* – because), Yahowah (efei) will not (*lo'*) forgive or leave unpunished (*raqah* – free from guilt, exempt from judgment and sentencing, pardon or release) those who relationally (*'eth 'asher*) deceive, beguile, or delude (*nasa'* – advance, lift up, support, bear, or desire, forgive or dignify, respect or tolerate / using clever trickery to mislead), in association with (*'eth* – through), His name (*shem* – renown and reputation) to promote and effect (*la* – accordingly) vain and ineffectual lies which lead to lifelessness and destruction (*shav'* / *show'* – devastating deceptions which nullify our existence leading to emptiness, worthlessness, and nothingness, deceitful, desolate, futile, and ruinous vanity)." (*Shemowth* / Names / Exodus 20:7)

Genesis 49:27 ESV
"Benjamin is a ravenous wolf, in the morning devouring the prey and at evening dividing the spoil."

If you do not devour some prey when you are young, you will have nothing to divide when you are old…. the Bible speaks of **devouring the prey in the morning so that in the evening you may divide the spoils.**

In this series I've been talking about Christ…. Who is He, not Who **was** He, but Who **IS He**? In this series I have been teaching about how the Old Testament is so critically important to the telling of the Story of Christ. Read on to understand why.

I've heard good people many times say that *'I just NEED a better harvest of Faith in my life; I need a better understanding of Spiritual things. I want to know Jesus! I want to understand Yeshua!'*

The unpleasant but immutable fact is this, in order to RECEIVE a better understanding of Christ, **you** must plant the seeds.

The Truth of this World, and the great Jim Rohn rightly said, *"Don't bring me your NEED, bring me your SEED!*

- What have you sown?
- What have you planted?
- How is it you bring me this great need, and yet you've planted no seeds?

- You've sown nothing, yet you want this great abundant Harvest.
- If you have a great need, then you had better get about planting great seed!"

People often mistakenly think that once you place your faith in Christ that everything, including learning about Christ will become easy that you won't really have anything to do but believe... even your faith can be on the fence.... We of course can have doubts about things.... This is what many believe.

More often than not, that errant belief is born from bad or more pleasant ear tickling teaching. As a preacher it is easier to warm an audience to move their feet at the altar call, it is easier for those seeking to walk down the aisle during the invitation if the preacher portrays the path and journey of Faith as one which is easy, smooth, clear.

Oh, a motivational *"spreacher"* can get resounding shouting Amens if they preach about the smooth easy path, but that isn't the Truth!

If you want to go forth and be fruitful, you better have some seed!

There's an entire generation of Christians who are always asking what they think is a philosophical theological question, *"How do I know God's will for my life? How do I know the will of God for my life?"*

Are you an avid reader? I know I am... in fact, I will admit, I am a book geek and I love to read!

Your seed might be that you are an avid reader, if that is the case, get about reading the Bible above not to the exclusion of all other literature.

If you are not a great reader but you love instructional videos or audio books.... Find some great, instructive Biblical videos and powerful audio books and get to watching, listening and sowing!

My point is this, If you want and need a vibrant Spiritual life and a REAL Relationship with Yeshua, you must must must find your seed!

How best Do I learn and grow?

Answer **that** question, then you will know your seed. Then, once you know your seed, You must SOW it! PLANT it! Watch it! Water it! Guard it from the bugs and the heat and the cold and the disease of this world! Not once and done, but every day...

You cannot reap a great and useful abundance if you do not plant vast amounts of the RIGHT seed for your unique soil!

We cannot know Christ, as we are intended until we begin to realize our unique role in the harvest!

Have you ever thought about the fact that God never made a table or a chair, but He sure does CREATE the trees!?

Do you understand that? God will not come into your new Christian life and make everything just so fluffy such that you will easily and without proper effort KNOW Him.

God doesn't make furniture. No! But God does make the Trees! It is up to US to imagine and build the tables and chairs and that takes work, OUR work!

The Trees are used to make paper... and on that paper God ordained it such that we have Divinely inspired Scripture to read any time we WANT and do!

Now, in the modern high-tech times, God gave us the firmament, and in that firmament God left it to us to put the satellites up into the galaxies so that the Internet can deliver His word, and the Work of His Son All around the world!

Incidentally, Do you know why porn is so prevalent on the Internet? Porn is so prevalent on the Internet, the World Wide Web because all of the space on the Internet IS NOT occupied with things of God.... Lovely things. You say, "But the Internet is infinite!"

No, the Internet isn't infinite…

But God is.

He gave us the Firmament and He empowered us with a brain such that we can read the Bible from our phones and iPads, from our computers, onto a little tiny iPod!

What I am saying to you is this; however you learn best, whatever harvesting tools you HAVE, **USE** them!

God doesn't birth our *hunger and thirst for Righteousness* based on what we do not already have, or can obtain, or learn or acquire. God will not direct us to NEED something that we cannot obtain, learn, or acquire from our current or available resources.

You need to SOW!

Some of your habits, you will need to reject and jettison in order to truly know and find knowledge of the King, the Lord of lords.

If you truly realize your NEED to search out God, and His Holy Spirit in your life, it ISN'T about what things or stuff you need **to go get**. No, it is most often about what you are willing to **let go of, what you are willing to jettison**.

The Truth is, you are going to have to let go of some things that you really do not want to let go, to leave some things and some people you love behind, you are going to have to do without some things you'd otherwise enjoy without a second thought.

Remember, it isn't about what you need, but what you are willing to let go!

Those things you won't release your *death grip* from will not bring you closer to Christ… Why do you think they call it a '*death grip?*'

The Spirit of the Living God will not be as present in you, or even at all if you are more concerned with, and more focused upon your pleasures in life, your distractions, your hurts habits and hang-ups instead of the time and effort, the focus and discipline to study the Word.... To pray the prayers.... To focus on what you have available to what you have right now and right here!

Until you shut off the distractions of the winds and rains beating upon your farm tractor windshield and get to planting seed early in the morning, in the afternoon, in the evening, and plowing away at the study and meditation on His Word.... All you will hear is the maddening noise and endless clatter of a raucous lost world.

It takes discipline to tune out the noise of the world to study... to find your seeds....

Did you know that not all of the Old Testament Believers believed in Hamashiach, the Messiah?

They couldn't quite conceive of the death, burial and Resurrection of Yeshua for their sins.... Don't be too hard on those early saints because we, in the modern age have the benefit of recorded History and the Bible, and Commentaries, and books like the one you now hold, and to be fair, many modern folk do not fully believe. They are on the fence despite all of the phenomenal faith tools at their disposal.

In contrast, the New Testament Saints and Teachers realized this very fact and component of Faith that we must believe in and on the resurrected Christ so that we will be saved!

They also realized that speaking of this belief in the resurrection this would cost many of them their very lives!

Romans 10:9 *But the righteousness based on faith says, "Do not say in your heart, 'Who will ascend into heaven?'"* (That is, to bring Christ down) *"or 'Who will descend into the abyss?'"* (that is, to bring Christ up from the dead). *But what does it say? "The word is near you, in your mouth and in* *your heart"* (that is, the word of faith that we proclaim); *because, if you confess with your mouth that Jesus is Lord and believe in your heart that God raised him from the dead, you will be saved. For with the heart one believes and is justified, and with the mouth one confesses and is saved. For the Scripture says, "Everyone who believes in him will not be put to shame." For there is no distinction between Jew and Greek; for the same Lord is Lord of all, bestowing his riches on all who call on him. For "everyone who calls on the name of the Lord will be saved."*

How then will they call on him in whom they have not believed? And how are they to believe in him of whom they have never heard? And how are they to hear without someone preaching? And how are they to preach unless they are sent? As it is written, "How beautiful are the feet of those who preach the good news!"

1 Corinthians 15:1-6
Now I would remind you, brothers, of the gospel I preached to you, which you received, in which you stand, and by which you are being saved, if you hold fast to the word I preached to you—unless you believed in vain.

For I delivered to you as of first importance what I also received: that Christ died for our sins in accordance with the Scriptures, that he was buried, that he was raised on the third day in accordance with the Scriptures, and that he appeared to Cephas, then to the twelve. Then he appeared to more than five hundred brothers at one time, most of whom are still alive, though some have fallen asleep.

Would you DIE for a LIE?

So then, we must ask, when and how did the Twelve Apostles die?

Summary: (This is a combination of my writing and some from an Internet search that for some reason I cannot replicate or credit. When I find the original poster, I will place attribution post haste.)

The Bible only mentions the deaths of two apostles, **James** who was put to death by Herod Agrippa I in 44 AD and **Judas Iscariot** who committed suicide shortly after the death of Christ.

The details of the deaths of three of the apostles (John, the Beloved, Bartholomew and Simon the Canaanite) are not known at all, either by tradition or early historians.

The deaths of the other seven apostles are known by tradition or the writings of early Christian historians.

According to traditions and the Bible, eight of the Apostles died as Martyrs.

At least two of the Apostles, Peter and Andrew were crucified.

Simon Called Peter by Christ died 33-34 years after the death of Christ. According to Smith's Bible Dictionary, there is "satisfactory evidence that he and Paul were the founders of the church at Rome and died in that city. The time and manner of the apostle's martyrdom are less certain. According to the early writers, he died at or about the same time with Paul, and in the Neronian persecution, A.D. 67,68. All agree that he was crucified.

Remember when I mentioned Origen? Origen said that Peter felt himself to be unworthy to be put to death in the same manner as his Master, and was, therefore, at his request, crucified with his head downward."

James the son of Zebedee: He was put to death by Herod Agrippa I shortly before the day of the Passover, in the year 44 or about 11 years after the death of Christ. From Acts 12: 1-2.

John: No death date given by early writers. Death date is by conjecture only and is variously assigned as being between 89 AD to 120 AD

Andrew: No accurate death date given. A variety of traditions say he preached in Scythia, in Greece, in Asia Minor and Thrace. He is reported to have been crucified at Patrae in Achaia.

Philip: Again, the Bible does not say when he died nor do we have accurate information. According to tradition, he preached in Phrygia and died at Hierapolis. Update: FoxNews July 27, 2011, Tomb of the Apostle Phillip is found in Hierapolis.

Bartholomew: There is no information concerning his death, not even by tradition

Matthew: He must have lived many years as an apostle since he was the author of the Gospel of Matthew, which was written at least twenty years after the death of Christ. There is a reason to believe that he stayed for fifteen years at Jerusalem, after which he went as a missionary to the Persians, Parthians and Medes. There is a legend that he died a martyr in Ethiopia.

Thomas: The earlier traditions, as believed in the fourth century, say he preached in Parthia or Persia and was finally buried at Edessa. The later traditions carry him farther east. His martyrdom whether in Persia or India, is said to have been by a lance. And is commemorated by the Latin Church on December 21 the Greek Church on October 6, and by the Native Americans on July 1.

James Alpheus: We know he lived at least five years after the death of Christ because of mentions in the Bible. According to tradition, the scribes and Pharisees threw James son of Alpheus down from the temple; he was then stoned, and his brains dashed out with a fuller's club.

Simon the Canaanite – No information either in the Bible or by tradition.

Jude (Thaddeus): according to tradition Jude taught in Armenia, Syria and Persia where he was martyred. Tradition tells us he was buried in Kara Kalisa in what is now Iran.

As you can discern, Following the Way closely, tightly, without apology may cost you your life. I know the Lord Yeshua Himself knew this cost first hand.

Yes, there is a great cost for Following Yeshua Hamashiach. There is cost for NOT denying Christ. You know what though, there is also a cost for rejecting Christ as Lord and Savior. Judas chose his path... He chose his seed of greed.

Judas Iscariot: Shortly after the death of Christ Judas killed himself. According to the Bible he hanged himself, (Matthew 27:5) at Aceldama, on the southern slope of the valley of Hinnom, near Jerusalem, and in the act he fell down a precipice and was dashed into pieces.

However you might be wondering if I can articulate and testify to what is the benefit of giving your life to Christ... I can... At this stage of my life especially, I can definitely tell you and the radio audience around the world that being a Follower of the Way doesn't make me perfect.

In fact, if you've known me for more than five minutes, you will know firsthand that I am very much just a regular dude.... I will tell you this, I know that I know that I know, when I close my eyes the last that I will look forever upon the Risen reason I am Redeemed! For all eternity, Redeemed by the shed blood of the Lamb!

But But But, Dr. Shawn!!! What about the benefit of believing in Yeshua TODAY!? That's great that when I die I am going to Heaven and I will be with Yeshua, but what about TODAY?!

How then shall we live here and now?

1. We Are Saved.

Salvation is the general term that the Bible uses to describe the miracle of grace God performs for us. It is the greatest event in our life. It has three main aspects or stages: past, present and future (cf. 2 Cor. 1:10). We were saved at a point in the past. This is when we were born again;

we believed, repented of sin, and were justified. It happens only once (born again, not born again and again and again). It is perfect and complete. We were rescued from danger, delivered from harm. Now we are saved and safe. Second, we are being saved in the present. Christ's blood keeps us safe from the wrath of God and He daily rescues us from Satan. Third, we will be saved in the future, at death and at the Judgment Day. These three stages are inseparable.

2. The Holy Spirit Indwells Us.

The Spirit enters the believer at the moment of regeneration and never leaves. He enters our whole being, even our body. It is the heavenly counterpart to being demon-possessed. He fills us. Romans 8 is the great chapter on the indwelling of the Spirit. Also, this is the miracle of the baptism of the Spirit, misunderstood by Pentecostals. The Spirit comes into us, with the result that He is in us. At the same moment, he puts us into Himself, with the result that we are in the Spirit. He is in us, and we are in Him.

It is not a second experience, but part of salvation. From there, we are to walk in the Spirit, go on being filled with the Spirit, etc.

3. The Christian Knows God.

Every person knows that God exists (Rom. 1), but only the Christian knows God personally. This is true knowledge. It is a heart-to-heart personal relationship. It is part of having eternal life (John 17:3). God granted us this privilege (Matt. 11:27). We know Him because He first knew us (I Cor. 8:3, Gal. 4:9). It is a personal, deep and intimate knowledge. We are friends. We are also lovers. And we grow in this knowledge deeper and deeper (Phil. 3:8, 10).

4. We are united to Christ.

This is similar to the union of the Holy Spirit. We are put into Christ's Body (I Cor. 12), with the result that we are "in Christ". At the same moment, Christ is put into us and is in us. In one sense, we were united with Him in the eternal Covenant, but we were united with Him in our experience when we were saved. We are united to Him and draw life from Him, and cannot do anything without Him (John 15). We are also united with Him in spiritual espousals. We are engaged to be His bride. One day, this will be consummated at the great heavenly marriage.

5. We are adopted into God's Family.

Once we were children of the Devil. God took us out of that family and made us His own children. Now God is our Father, other believers are our brothers and sisters, and Christ is our elder brother. Being His children, we are also His heirs. We can now call God "our Father in Heaven". Adoption is not the same as regeneration. Regeneration affects our nature; adoption affects our relationship. Regeneration precedes faith, which precedes adoption. But it happens in a moment, with no interval or exception. So, we are doubly God's children.

6. We Are Reconciled to God.

This is a great benefit of salvation that we often overlook. 2 Cor. 5 is the great chapter on it. We were once God's enemies; now we are His friends. We are reconciled. It is more than a truce; it is the end of hostilities. The war is over. We have peace with God. We were once against God and God against us. Now He is for us and with us, and we with Him. Properly speaking, it is we that are reconciled to God, not God to us. We apologize, not He. Yet, on His part, the righteous enmity was removed when His wrath was appeased when Christ died for us.

7. We Are No Longer Under Wrath.

We were once sinners under the wrath of God - condemned, doomed, facing judgment. All that has changed. We will never be judged. God is not angry with us, but smiles on us in Fatherly love. God saved us from several things: sin, Satan, death, Hell. But most importantly, He saved us from His own wrath. God saved us from God. Lost sinners are still under His wrath (John 3:36). But not us. As fierce as His wrath was against us then, so intense is His love for us now.

8. We Are Cleansed From Sin.

Our sins were filthy and disgusting. Even our religious acts were filthy rags. But God changed all that. He cleansed us (I Cor. 6:11). He washed away the black guilt by the blood of Christ. We were baptized in the blood of the Lamb. Our sins were drowned in the Red Sea of His blood. Only Christ's blood, not the waters of baptism, can cleanse us in this way, for water cannot touch the soul. In one sense, we are already totally cleansed. In another, we need daily cleansing for the regular sins we commit (see John 13). This does not mean we get saved all over again. It only means that we need fresh applications of the blood of Christ (I John 1:7).

9. We Are Transferred From Satan's Kingdom.

Col. 1:13 says that God transferred us from the kingdom of darkness into the kingdom of light. Christ, not Satan, is now our King. We defected from Satan's evil empire, became traitors to his wicked regime, and now are God's spies engaged in espionage and commandoes involved in sabotage. We have been rescued from Satan's claws; he cannot ever have us again. We are on another team, part of another body, having different allegiances. We were once for Satan and against God; now we are against Satan and for God (Matt. 6:24). If God is for us, who can be against us?

10. We Cannot Lose Our Salvation.

One of the great glories of salvation is that it is permanent. It has a ratchet-effect. Once saved, always saved. It is not because of our own selves, or even our own faith. It is ultimately dependent on God, for it was He that saved us in the first place. If it depended on us, none of us would get saved or stay saved. God elected us to salvation (Rom. 8:29-30) and completes what He started (Phil. 1:6). He has sworn to preserve, keep and guard us forever (Psa. 37:28, 66:9, 97:10, 145:14, 20, I Tim. 1:12). He keeps us by His omnipotent hand (1 Pet. 1:5), keeps us safe from Satan (I John 5:18, John 17:11, 12, 15), and seals us with the Holy Spirit (Eph. 1:13, 4:30). The saints in Heaven are happier, but not more secure, than we are. Simply put, God loves His people too much to let them go. He holds us firmly and lovingly in His arms of love, from which no one can snatch us out (John 10:28).

THAT is what Yeshua did for me… and you… and those in this world who accept Him, AND His redemption…. Have you?

Now let us get back to the Old Testament story…

Book of the Bible – Leviticus (The Hebrew word is *wayyiqra* – meaning *"and He {the Lord} called."*
Author – 3rd Book of Moses
Date of Writing – Shortly after exodus from Egypt
Number of Chapters - 27
To Whom Written – The Hebrew Nation now Redeemed
Purpose of the Writing – To teach the redeemed nation how to live for, serve, and worship God. This is the book of laws and regulation of a people in a way that points to its ultimate fulfillment in Christ's crucifixion thereby granting a passage to God.

My Personal Summary–

This is a book of detailed instruction for the pursuit of holiness by sinful people.

At this point, sacrifice TO God was pre-eminent to sacrifice FOR God.

This Levitical system of intense regulations served as a seemingly complex path to full obedience to and pleasing of God.

We are sinful people and God is Holy and there must be a bridge between the two in order to bring about relationship.

At the time of writing, Leviticus served as that bridge until Christ came as the propitiation for our sins.

Sacrifices and offerings are discussed in Chapters 1-7. Priestly duties and requirements are discussed in Chapters 8-10. Cleanliness and holiness is instructed in Chapters 11-12. In order to comply with the litany of rules and laws I doubt anyone was actually ever truly *"clean."*

Finally, my favorite part; laws pertaining to feasts are directed in Chapter 23.

The last four chapters give the benefits and promises for keeping the law and the price for disobedience.

The theme of Leviticus may seem like an outdated treatment of rules and laws and legalistic manner of living for God. I recognize why one would come to that conclusion but if read repeatedly in the light of the cross, one realizes the great sacrifice, once and for all, that Yeshua the Christ provided with His shed blood for our sins. We must never forget the price paid for our freedom in Christ, which includes the rules and rituals contained within the Book of Leviticus.

Book of the Bible – Numbers (Hebrew title for this book is *Bemidbar –* meaning *"in the desert."*)
Author – Traditionally ascribed to Moses
Date of Writing – 1450-1410 B.C.
Number of Chapters - 36
To Whom Written – The people of Israel
Purpose of the Writing – Details the 38 years of journey that should have been an eleven-day walk – but disobedience made the pathway rocky and long.

My Personal Summary–

The Book of Numbers amplifies a theme, which rings very true today; "Believing in God is not enough. We must believe, trust, and obey God. The paths to God's will for our lives do not just involve obedience, it revolves around it! The sheer logistics of the forty-year wilderness journey stemming from disobedience, distrust and dishonoring of God points us toward a simpler way of living.

In our finite "wisdom" we translate what is actually simple into painful and costly complexity. We make a forty-year struggle out of an eleven-day walk!

We will experience life-challenges. We were never promised we would not go through lands of trial. We were also never told to stay in the land of trials either. Through obedience to God we find the map out of dry thirsty lands into a place of pure joy with God.

In Numbers 1-10 a census is taken and legislative instruction is given. The entire rest of the book is a record of mans failure to consult a map when lost. Numbers might record the first instance of, "be careful what you ask for!" It is clear the Israelites had needs. It is also clear that God met each of those needs. The struggle today seems to echo that of this time in that the grumbling and griping we do might be an indication of a rebellious spirit. It is easy to disguise our rebellious spirit with church vernacular or a certain type of behavior, but in the end, God knows our hearts and just how lost we are.

Book of the Bible – Deuteronomy
Greek "*To Deuteronomion Touto*" meaning in English; "*This Second Law.*"
Author - Moses
Date of Writing – 1407/6 B.C.
Number of Chapters - 34
To Whom Written – Israel (The new generation entering the Promised Land)
Purpose of the Writing – Joshua serves up a great reminder of what God did for them and to encourage them to rededicate their lives to God.

My Personal Summary–

This great book begins with a review of the Levitical Law more specifically directed toward regular people rather than just priests.

Chapter 1-4:43 review the Israelites history.

The Law is reviewed again in Chapter 4:44-26:19 amplifies just how important sacrificial and specific obedience really is.

The covenant with God's people is illuminated in the chapters and verses 27:1-30:20.

The *"curses"* of certain behavior is frightfully recorded in 27:11-26 contrasting with Chapter 28's promises of obedience.

Immediately following Chapter 28:14 to the end of Chapter 28 the price for disobedience is itemized in great detail.

The exhortation to the Israelites is very ominous as recorded in Ch. 28:58-68 and again in Ch. 30:11-30.

As ominous as it was, there are several words of encouragement offered to us as a testament to the guidance and protection of an eternal God. It is interesting that Moses died on a mountain overlooking all that God promised and delivered to Moses' people.

Moses was comparatively young and spry at 120 years old and yet his work on earth was finished and thus, he died and was buried in a secret location known only to God.

Could this be that despite his greatness, he was still a man and not to be worshipped? Or, did God know that the Devil would hate Moses so much that he would desecrate his grave?

Deuteronomy reminds us to reflect on God's goodness and provision in our lives spurring rededication to His will and way in our lives when the times get tough....

Book of the Bible – Joshua
Author - Joshua, with the exception of the ending which is believed to have been written by Phinehas; the high priest who witnessed the very events recounted in the book.
Date of Writing – 1407-1383 B.C.
Number of Chapters - 24
To Whom Written – The Nation of Israel
Purpose of the Writing – The conquest and division of the Land of Canaan

My Personal Summary–

Over the course of fifty years this bunch of whiners transforms into a nation with obedience and resolve to do God's perfect will.

Twelve distinctly separate but inarguably connected tribes serve to enact the will of God in the land of promise.

The key to this transformation is strong **and** <u>unquestioning</u> obedience of the Lord God by a leader who refused to compromise the direction of God.

Joshua was the man **God** <u>**ordained**</u> for this holy task; leading the people of Israel into the land of Canaan promised **to** <u>**them**</u>.

The swinging of the sword would be required of the Israelites because the people of Canaan were embroiled in ungodly behavior and as we know of God, He routes out evil by whatever means necessary, **including** <u>**killing**</u> the disobedient.

The title of this book of the Bible is in Hebrew; Hoshea or *"Salvation."* Our salvation comes in the form of obedience to God before He has to reprimand us, or we choose the more painful route of having to be corrected by God.

The Book of Joshua details several unique and miraculous events.

Those events include:

The River Jordan divided, 3:14-17 - Supernatural Intervention in **nature** to rescue an obedient people.

An angel appearing to Joshua, 5:13-15 - Supernatural Visitation from an Angel to point out to Joshua that he was **standing on Holy Ground**, consecrated by God Himself.

The walls of Jericho collapsing, 6:1-20 - Supernatural intervention in **re-engineering the physics** of human-made structures to make them fall without explosives.

The storm of hailstones, 10:11 - God **controlling** nature to affect the attention of His people.

The sun and the moon standing still, 10:12-14 – God's impact in our lives should be **Supernatural, unlimited**.

Book of the Bible – Judges or *Shophetim*: "rulers, judges, saviors."[1]
Author – Likely Samuel
Date of Writing – Precise date is unknown; however, the writing commences during the reign of Saul and continues for 350 years.
Number of Chapters – 21
To Whom Written – The Nation of Israel
Purpose of the Writing - Detailing the conversion of twelve tribes into one nation while reminding the reader that if we are disobedient to God, we are in trouble. Our judgment and deliverance comes not from human beings, but from God.

---

[1] John Hunt, comp., *The Ultimate Bible Outline Book: Every Book of the Bible Made Simple*, (Chattanooga, TN: AMG, 2006), WORD*search* CROSS e-book, 115.

My Personal Summary–

Book of the Bible – Judges or Shophetim: "rulers, judges, saviors."
Author – Likely Samuel
Date of Writing –Precise date is unknown; however, the writing commences during the reign of Saul and continues for 350 years.
Number of Chapters - 21
To Whom Written – The Nation of Israel
Purpose of the Writing – Detailing the **conversion** of twelve tribes into one nation while reminding the reader that if we are disobedient to God, we are in trouble.

Our judgment and deliverance comes not from human beings, **but** from God.

My Personal Summary–

In the process of becoming a nation instead of a compilation of twelve separate but related tribes, Israelites experience the searing wrath of God for their disobedience and the intense blessing and providence of a God Who is to be obeyed.

Only **by faith** are we **propelled** to our destiny **determined by God.**

The great faith of the people of God was rewarded with good times and a healthy period for the Israelites; however, the incident of Samson examines the contrasts of lifelong obedience of God, and the penalty for disobedience despite the lengthy obedience.

God is a just god.

The laying out of the fleece by Gideon who heard the Word of God in direction but he still needed *more **direction*** and "*proof.*" Most people point to the "*laying out of the fleece*" as a tool we should use today to disclose the will of God, yet they are terribly wrong. Faith is faith in *what we do not see* or know **by** clear physical evidence and the laying out of the fleece expresses doubt in God and our weak faith.

There are often **rash _vows_ offered** to God to rescue one from the place **of their own doing.** We make hasty vows as in Jephthah's rash vow, (Chapter 11:29-40) which resulted in him having to sacrifice his own dear daughter to honor what had to be one of the stupidest vows I have ever heard! If your only child is your dear daughter, why would you vow to sacrifice whoever would come to the door when you return?

Samson's incredible physical strength was most assuredly a gift directly and exclusively from God yet **he lost himself** in the mission of God through the temptations all men and women face. The Nation of Israel was in spiritual and moral decline shortly after their great leader, Joshua died. This to me echoes the importance of powerful and dependable spiritual leadership in the world, the nation, the home, the marriage, and the heart.

Book of the Bible – Ruth - From the Hebrew word *"reuit," which* means *"Friendship."*
Author – Likely Samuel though some commentaries place Ruth as one of two female writers of books of the Bible, the other being Ester.
Date of Writing – Precise date is unknown; however, the writing commences prior to Samuel
1046-1035 B.C.
Number of Chapters - 4
To Whom Written – The Nation of Israel
Purpose of the Writing – To show that a non-Jew was in the lineage of Jesus Christ and that consistent love and dedicate to one another and to God is rewarded.

My Personal Summary–

This often under-read book of the Bible is to me profoundly simple.

Consistent in her love, unwavering in her dedication to Naomi, Ruth is a love story for family, God, and obedience to God's Will and Word.

Ruth follows Naomi after Naomi's husband died even to the point of leaving her homeland to travel wherever Naomi would go.

Ruth adopted the people of Naomi and the people of Naomi adopted her.

In spite of the appearance of the situation being dire, Ruth became all action and very little talk by declaring that she would not leave Naomi.

Ruth knew how to work, and work she did. In the fields, in the home, on the way to work, Ruth worked hard.

God rewards consistent effort and dedication of His people and Ruth was richly rewarded by providing more than was mandated to provide. God provided overflow, more than Ruth could ever have imagined.

God gave Ruth a great man in Boaz who surely recognized great character in Ruth.

In so doing, God placed Ruth squarely in the lineage of Jesus Christ.

Doing good and kindness to others should not be motivated by our ambition for good to come to us as a result of our kindness.

Our intent should be to do well unto others, to honor our commitments, and to follow through on God's direction in our lives.

God blesses those *deserving* of blessings, as He did for Ruth. Obedience begets blessing and often blessings beget an obedient life.

Book of the Bible – 1 Samuel
Author – Samuel to Chapter 24, Nathan and Gad.
Gad (/gæd/) was a seer or prophet mentioned in the Hebrew Bible and the writings of Jewish historian Josephus. He was one of the personal

prophets of King David of Israel and, according to the Talmudic tradition; some of his writings are believed to be included in the Books of Samuel.
Date of Writing – 1011 B.C.
Number of Chapters - 31
To Whom Written – The nation of Israel
Purpose of the Writing – To record the founding of Hebrew monarchy

My Personal Summary–

This is the story of transfer of the land from judgeship to monarchy and kings. Samuel, the last of the judges mentors the first king, Saul while the destiny of Israel waits.

Hannah felt her bitterness was justified.

We might allow difficult circumstances to color our entire outlook on life or we can be blessed by God Who obviously provided for Hannah.

When others find our "hot button" they will push it repeatedly as Peninnah did. The less we whine, the less salt our detractors have to rub in our wounds.

Hannah learned this, as will we. (This is a free extra; Hannah is a palindrome, same word forward or back. You're welcomed!)

Samuel was in the unique position of mentoring the very first king of Israel but before he could mentor the king he had to listen and learn from godly men and women.

It is clear by his later leadership, Samuel learned well. Samuel was not present to hear the lament and depression of Hannah; however he was present to hear her great praises of thanksgiving to God for His meeting exceeding her wants.

Children hearing the praising of God within the home will beget greater results in our children than constant complaints against God.

In contrast, the lenience of Eli for his son's deplorable behavior costs his family greatly.

If a parent loves their children they will raise them up in the Lord's ways rather than today's postmodern penchant for allowing the children to decide for themselves who or what they will worship instead of imparting the admonition of the Lord.

Book of the Bible – 2 Samuel
Author – Unknown.
Date of Writing – After 973 b.c.
Number of Chapters - 24
To Whom Written – The nation of Israel
Purpose of the Writing – To record the history of David's reign, which foreshadowed Christ, the ideal leader of a new and perfect kingdom.

My Personal Summary–

Flawed men and women make up the Kingdom here on Earth.

David was flawed and yet he was not only a great leader, but also the progenitor of the lineage in which Jesus Christ would come.

In 1 Samuel the life of Sampson is presented as that of an incredibly strong man with obvious gifts from God, yet he faltered severely even unto his death because he disobeyed God, refusing to live in His will.

David sought to honor God but suffered greatly under temptation from women, disobedience, self-reliance, and anger.

David sinned greatly and he served God greatly, yet he was forgiven because he repented with intensity and sincere regret, and willingness to change.

God chose David because he could do great things and lead an entire people into battles, challenges, and their destiny determined by God.

David was tormented by temptation yet he is said to have sought the heart of God. We may be that way at times but the question is, how do we "finish?"

David's life was a roller coaster; however, he always sought to honor God and give God the glory for his victories, David also was a strategic thinker who was very well organized.

This is important for the king of a young nation to be able to do; to organize a previously scattered people. The difference between David and many other kings is that David sought to organize his people under God.

Under God the king and his people prospered. Outside of God they starved physically and spiritually.

Book of the Bible – 1 Kings
Author – Unknown.
Date of Writing – Shortly before 587 B.C.
Number of Chapters - 22
To Whom Written – The nation of Israel
Purpose of the Writing – To detail the impact and division of the Kingdom of Israel due to the moral and spiritual decline of their people <u>and kings.</u>

My Personal Summary–

David served <u>his purpose</u> to God despite his repeated disobedience and when it was time, a new king would assume the throne. Solomon was a wise king, but he too was extravagant and subject to temptations that befell him and lesser men. Solomon inherited from his father David a peaceful nation as a result of conquests of King David's fulfillment of God's destiny for him, almost.

Solomon had a destiny from God as well, and he too was seriously challenged with moral dilemmas and failures. In obedience to God Solomon was permitted to ask of God anything and he asked for wisdom and understanding, which God granted.

This gifting was empowered so long as Solomon obeyed God. A simple disobedience such as buying horses from Egypt would have long-term implications and ramifications for not only Solomon, but also his family.

Solomon was obedient and detailed in fulfilling what his father David was charged to do by God; "Build My temple!"

It is foreign for today's secular worldview to reconcile the need for a stunning temple to point toward Yahweh yet it is customary to build elaborate sports facilities or stunning mansions and grounds.

Despite being in God's Will, Solomon was hungry to accumulate beautiful women from Israel and other lands who then influenced Solomon into paganism, which was a clear violation of God's direction.

Solomon is said to be the wisest and wealthy man on Earth yet the simplest temptation felled his full impact. Even the wisest and wealthiest may fall.

Book of the Bible – 2 Kings
Author – Unknown.
Date of Writing – Shortly before 587 B.C. except for chapters 2 Kings 24-25 which were written about 550 B.C.
Number of Chapters - 25
To Whom Written – The nation of Israel
Purpose of the Writing – To provide an historical account of the kingdoms of Israel and Judah, from the latter part of the reign of Ahaziah in Israel, and Jehoram in Judah, up to the time of the captivities.

Also, to provide evidence of what happens to the leaders and a nation of people that defies God.

My Personal Summary–

Elijah performed many miracles to authenticate the movement of God. Some of those miracles are:

(1) Elijah's word stops the rains. <u>1 Kings 17:1</u>
(2) Elijah's promise multiplies a widow's food. <u>1 Kings 17:14</u>
(3) Elijah's prayer restores the widow's son to life. <u>1 Kings 17:21</u>
(4) Elijah's prayer calls down fire on Mount Carmel. <u>1 Kings 18:38</u>
(5) Elijah's word restores rain to the land. <u>1 Kings 18:41</u>
(6) Elijah calls down fire on soldiers. <u>2 Kings 1:12</u>
(7) Elijah divides waters of the Jordan. <u>2 Kings 2:8</u>

Despite these miracles Elijah would be taken to Heaven without dying and without seeing complete obedience of the people. Interestingly enough, Jesus also came, lived perfection, died and rose again and yet the people did not believe.

Elijah asked of Elisha what he would like in 2 Kings 2:9 and Elisha asked for a double portion of grace be upon him, and it apparently was granted in light of the many miracles performed by Elisha after the fire chariots translated Elijah to Heaven.

God always provides a new leader when a leader dies or moves on to another mission.

God always deals with idol worshippers. Harshly.

His wrath is never light though many place their boats, vacations, homes, their jobs, even their appearance above God and God will deal with all of us who might place anything above worshipping Him.

Sometimes obedience to God for our healing is dirty business as it was for Naaman dipping seven times in the Jordan River for release from Leprosy. Elisha said God said seven times, and no miracle in part or whole came until the rising out of the water the seventh time. This is a powerful lesson for complete obedience to God.

Book of the Bible – 1 Chronicles
Author – Unknown, though Ezra is thought to have been an editor.
Date of Writing – Between 450 and 430 B.C.
Number of Chapters - 29
To Whom Written – The nation of Israel
Purpose of the Writing – To provide a spiritual perspective of events from David's reign to the decree of Cyrus in 538 B.C.; and, to illustrate the absolute importance of national and personal worship.

My Personal Summary–

It has been said, *"One cannot know his destination until one knows from where he came."* Most people skip the endless genealogies in this book. I am guilty of that.

Chapters 1-9 detail the people from whom our Jesus and we are descended. What could be more important? Chapter 10 details the death of Saul by his own hand as a result of an archer's arrow.

Saul killed himself rather than being taken alive by the enemies, yet they cut off his head and hung it on the wall of the Temple of Dagon.

Soldiers risked their lives to retrieve the head of a great soldier, king, and leader but why? Because he sinned against God by consulting a Medium Saul died at his own hand.

Saul, one who trusted God eschewed the counsel of God in trade for the counsel of men of Satan. What a change of direction!

It is interesting how God, upon the total faith and request of His people, especially His prophets, leaders, and kings will grant a clear path. This path will not always be smooth, but God will make it straight and clear. Perhaps we have not seen the miracles of old because our faith is so small and untidy?

The faith of our ancestors was sporadic though, as we see from Saul contacting a Medium for advice rather than God Himself.

It seems odd to me that if he could directly seek the direction of God, why would he talk to a mortal?

The real question is, why do we?

Book of the Bible – 2 Chronicles
Author – Unknown, though Ezra is thought to have been an editor.
Date of Writing – Between 450 and 430 B.C.
Number of Chapters - 36
To Whom Written – The nation of Israel
Purpose of the Writing – Showing the contrast of good and obedient Kings and the sinful Kings, the spotlight is placed upon the role of true worship in the life of the believer.

My Personal Summary–

Solomon was the son of David that was to assume the crown from his dying father and he was quite a military, diplomacy, economic policy and architectural genius. However; he must have been a forerunner of the democrats because he believed in taxing the people so heavily they could hardly bear the burden and pleaded for relief. In addition, the conscripts; both Israeli and foreigners deeply resented forced service to the king.

We are told Solomon was a man of prayer and deep relationship with God and it follows that God's Hand was upon him as he served Him and did God's Will. God recognizes our hearts intent, good or bad. Chapter 6, Verse 1-11 truly highlights God's recognition of David's heart and it reminds me that He sees my heart too.

2Ch 6:1 Then Solomon said, "The Lord has said that He would dwell in the thick cloud.

2 "I have built You a lofty house, And a place for Your dwelling forever."

3 Then the king faced about and blessed all the assembly of Israel, while all the assembly of Israel was standing.

4 He said, "Blessed be the Lord, the God of Israel, who spoke with His mouth to my father David and has fulfilled it with His hands, saying,

5 'Since the day that I brought My people from the land of Egypt, I did not choose a city out of all the tribes of Israel in which to build a house that My name might be there, nor did I choose any man for a leader over My people Israel;

6 but I have chosen Jerusalem that My name might be there, and I have chosen David to be over My people Israel.'

7 "Now it was in the heart of my father David to build a house for the name of the Lord, the God of Israel.

8 "But the Lord said to my father David, 'Because it was in your heart to build a house for My name, you did well that it was in your heart.(Emphasis mine)

9 'Nevertheless you shall not build the house, but your son who will be born to you, he shall build the house for My name.'

10 "Now the Lord has fulfilled His word which He spoke; for I have risen in the place of my father David and sit on the throne of Israel, as the Lord promised, and have built the house for the name of the Lord, the God of Israel.

11 "There I have set the ark in which is the covenant of the Lord, which He made with the sons of Israel."

In verse 7 Solomon acknowledges that which his father David lived, though not perfectly. In Verse 8 the Lord Himself recognizes what was in David's heart as it relates to God was good and his intent was good. David was recognized by Solomon in his prayer. This does not mean God endorses unfulfilled intent (*"I tried to do well, I wanted to do well!"*) as "good enough."

"You meant well" is not expressed by God. God knows the root of our hearts though God's mercy is not bound by that knowledge. Throughout 2 Chronicles we see several more examples of leaders who knew better, but didn't do better.

2Ch 26:4 He did right in the sight of the Lord according to all that his father Amaziah had done.

5 He continued to seek God in the days of Zechariah, who had understanding through the vision of God; and as long as he sought the Lord, God prospered him.

2 Chronicles 7:13-14 (TLV) 13 If I shut up heaven that there is no rain, or if I command the locust to devour the land, or if I send pestilence among My people, 14 when My people, over whom My Name is called, humble themselves and pray and seek My face and turn from their evil ways, then I will hear from heaven and will forgive their sin and will heal their land.

Book of the Bible - Ezra

Author – Ezra

Date of Writing – 440 B.C.

Number of Chapters - 10

To Whom Written – The Israelites

Purpose of the Writing – Documentation of the return of the exiles and the genealogy of those returning. In addition, to document the sins of the people and the restoration in God.

My Personal Summary–

Who returned and how many came? Ezra answers this question with detailed lists and indexes, which tells us who comprised the Nation of Israel post-exilic.

Truth be told, In years past I would have skipped The Old Testament Book of the Bible, Ezra due to the boring nature of the lists and genealogy details however, as I grew more mature as a follower of The Way, I learned the Book of Ezra has great power within its chapters.

The power of this great book is replete with exhortations for purity and purification of that which was previously defiled in order to restore worship of THE Holy God.

This is a great lesson for the Post Modern Western Evangelical Worldview of today in that people are too comfortable with Yeshua such that the hip trendy and cool speak to and about The Savior of the World as though Jesus Christ were one of their school friends.

The impurity spoken of early on in the book is that of the priests who took wives from prohibited sources.

You see, they could maintain plural wives, but the wives had to be from very specific sources.

In this day and age it seems anything goes, though in the time of the writing of Ezra, that was hardly the case.

Now, for clarification, let me make this distinction…. I am often asked what I think of Bethel Music and Worship and other similar groups. I am asked, *"Do you think they are genuine, legitimate, scripturally accurate, and not just a money making scheme?"*

I answer this way…. I cannot know their hearts. I cannot measure them because it isn't my place. I can tell you this; I grew up on Conservative Hymns and no clapping or saying amen after a good song or sermon.

It was a KJV Authorized Version only growing up time.

Then, when Gaither Vocal Band, Carmen, Sandi Patty, Larnell Harris, and similar gained popularity, they were portrayed as disrespectful and an abomination to "good Christian respectful worship." Then, when Stryper and Petra came out, the world might as well have been ending!

The world hadn't yet heard of Christian Rap. That would have been apocalyptic back then! There is now an entire Christian Broadcasting System, Satellite Radio, the Internet, and more. I've spoken about this for many years…

My conclusion is this; there are some, which are genuine, and following, hard after God… and some are not. I can tell you this; Christian Music is changing, and will keep changing…. Seek past the rhythm and beats and listen to the lyrics…. Dig down deep in the lyrics. Lauren Daigle has taken a lot of heat from "Good Christian Folk" because she doesn't come down hard on LGBT people.

You must remember this; Lauren Daigle is in her faith where she is… not where she was, or where she will be…. Neither are we. We all go through fire and flame…. We win and we fail. We rise, we fall…. And we get up, or we don't. What I know is this; Lauren Daigle is reaching millions of people that I will never reach, millions of radio listeners or not. They will HEAR her when they would never HEAR me. The gospel is being spread.

We must not confuse our personal preferences with failing to honor God.... We cannot say that something is not "God honoring" simply because we don't like a particular style of music. The same refers to church styles of worship, or styles of Houses of Worship... But, in the original places of Worship, the True House of God, there were very specific commandments... Requirements, not recommendations. Why? Because there was no applicable or relevant precedent.

The *"House of the Lord"* was to be rebuilt and though the resources of Solomon were no longer available, an honorable restoration began.

In my time, the revealed purpose and value of a respected house of worship has come under attack by ACTUAL enemies of our faith, the practice of our faith, though we know now, through Jesus Christ, that it isn't a particular style of building, rather, **we** are the church, though we rarely act that way.

Zerubbabel was clear in his mission to rebuild the temple and who and how they were to rebuild this temple! Even whom you were married to mattered to God.

Book of the Bible - Nehemiah
Author - Ezra
Date of Writing – 430 B.C.
Number of Chapters - 13
To Whom Written – The Israelites
Purpose of the Writing – Since Ezra and Nehemiah are thought to have been presented in one book in the original Hebrew text, this is believed to be a restatement and confirmation of the facts in Ezra. Nehemiah goes a bit further into detail in some areas that Ezra either addresses lightly, or not at all.

My Personal Summary–

I am a preacher who preaches forty-five minutes to an hour or more and Chapter 8 of Nehemiah is one of my favorite passages for reasons you will soon see.

> *Ne 8:1 And all the people gathered as one man at the square which was in front of the Water Gate, and they asked Ezra the scribe to bring the book of the law of Moses which the Lord had given to Israel. ²Then Ezra the priest brought the law before the assembly of men, women and all who could listen with understanding, on the first day of the seventh month. ³He read from it before the square, which was in front of the Water Gate from early morning until midday, in the presence of men and women, those who could understand; and <u>all the people were attentive</u> to the book of the law. (Emphasis mine) ⁴Ezra the scribe stood at a wooden podium, which they had <u>made for the purpose.</u>(First raised pulpit ever.)*

In review of the Hebrew calendar it is clear that in this part of the world, it was unbearably hot and yet they stood from early morning to midday 127 degrees Fahrenheit.

Post Modern Western Evangelical Society and many seminaries; tell us that sermons longer than twenty-minutes cannot be tolerated by the majority of the congregation.

Why are church chairs and pews padded? Because they are meant to be comfortable, so we can sit a little longer than 20 minutes than at the ballgames we regularly attend for 4 hours? Why is temperature control in houses of worship so important? Because keeping the people comfortable is critically important…. Nowadays.

Yet, in the desert heat, for hours, these people stood and listened silently to the Word. Perhaps we aren't receiving the blessing of reclamation of God in our lives because we are unwilling to endure any discomfort for the sake of relationship with God. Maybe we should worry less about the authenticity and appropriateness of Lauren Daigle, and more of our own?

Perhaps our dedication to our Faith and our God, rather than our attention spans should be questioned?

> *Ne 8: 5Ezra opened the book in the sight of all the people for he was standing above all the people; and when he opened it, all the people stood up.(Emphasis mine.) 6Then Ezra blessed the Lord the great God. And all the people answered, "Amen, Amen!" while lifting up their hands; then they bowed low and worshiped the Lord with their faces to the ground.*

Respect for God's Word is nearly lost in this *"Me"* generation. Men and women have bled and died to bring us this book and yet many people have no concept of its value. Further, the importance of covenants in this society seems nearly lost.

People make "deals" and then renege on those covenants regularly. Chapter 9 Verse 38 speaks of an in-writing agreement that was signed by Nehemiah the Governor and many others, but God bound the covenant.

The signers and obligors or this document were binding themselves to God to be cursed should they fail to complete the agreement with Almighty God. The covenant was clear, yet some still violated the agreement as do we, Christians fully aware of what is expected of us. Thank God He is the God of mercy through Jesus' blood.

"ADONAI bless you and keep you! ADONAI make His face to shine on you and be gracious to you! ADONAI turn His face toward you and grant you shalom!" — Numbers 6:24-26 TLV

'Something Sacred hangs in the balance of every moment'. Heschel.

"In a classroom full of students, a professor asks:

If you had $86,400.00 and someone stole $10.00 from you, would you throw away the $86,390.00 you still have to try and get your $10.00 back? Or would you just let it go?

They all said they would let it go. So would I.

Then he told them, you have 86,400 seconds every single day and this time is much more valuable than money. You can always work for more money, but once a second pass you can never get it back.

Every time someone upsets us, it probably took 10 seconds, so why do we throw away the other 86,390 seconds worrying about it or being upset??

We all make this mistake and it is time to start letting the "little things go." You can do it. I believe in you!!"

My name is Dr. Shawn Michael Greener and I'm here to tell you, Today is a GREAT day to be ALIVE!

Book of the Bible - Esther
Author - Unknown
Date of Writing – 460 B.C.
Number of Chapters - 9
To Whom Written – The Jewish people
Purpose of the Writing – To record the institution of the annual festival of Purim and to document yet another deliverance of the Israelites by God

My Personal Summary–

The curious absence of clear references to God, YHWH or even the LORD is what stands out most profoundly when I first read Esther. However, when I re-read the book I am impressed with the detailed accounts of events that enter the life of Esther and the fact that somehow, she trusts that all will be okay.

The steps Esther takes to rescue her homeland from destruction by risking her palatial lifestyle in the royal court, and even her life.

Esther was certainly not in a position to loathe her station in life. She had a lifestyle of privilege and in a sense, freedom while not yet free. Esther had a secret and within that secret she hid all of who she is, a Jew.

That was not simply her nationality by birth, it was her very identity and to deny her Jewishness is to deny herself.

This; being a Jew, was who and what she was, despite her finery that she wore, and the splendor that she lived within, Esther was in the same house as Jesus Christ, the house of the Jews, the Hebrew nation.

In the very end of the book of Esther the mention of Mordecai's standing among not only men, but also among Jewish kings is a bit surprising; however, within the mission and will of God nothing is impossible.

The key as revealed in Esther is that we must first obey God, <u>and then</u> He will unveil His perfect will for our lives and not before.

Book of the Bible - Job
Author - Moses
Date of Writing – Approximately 2000-1800 B.C.
Number of Chapters - 42
To Whom Written – The Hebrew people <u>and</u> all nations that follow.
Purpose of the Writing – Why do the righteous suffer and the evil prosper?

This book answers this burning and enduring question and it addresses what authentic and more importantly, faith which is tested looks like, and lives like, and maybe dies like…

My Personal Summary–

- Thought to be the first written book of the Bible, this is a beautiful account of Job and his family going through the most awful suffering I have ever contemplated without relief of death.

Job's faith is more than circumstance-deep as is the case with many Christians in the world today. I learned a very powerful and enduring lesson my own suffering.. If I wait for circumstances to bring me happiness, I might be waiting for a long time for something that may never come.

Especially given the climate of prosperity preaching and the post modern emergent philosophy focusing more upon what we can get from God, rather than what we should give to God; our unremitting obedience despite our life circumstances.

Trusting God and obeying God despite the worldly view of our lives is difficult and no book better demonstrates this challenge than Job.

In Job's life everything seemed to be well and wealth and family was congruent with Job's reverence with God.

Job often made sacrifices, not just for himself, but also for his family.

Job was serious about his obedience and reverence for God, unlike much of the church today.

Job's friends came and sat with him, silently as in the Hebrew tradition to grieve silently until the sufferer speaks.

When these men came and sat with the suffering Job knew they meant well, but did not do well. In fairness to these men, many of us would approach a friend in great suffering and ask them if they have any un-confessed sin?

God rebuked Job's friends and in the end, Job was doubly restored. I can only imagine how much deeper his relationship is with the God he so devoutly obeyed having come through this crucible of faith.

Job's Tests and Satan's Goal from an entry https://www. evangelicaloutreach.org/jobtest.htm
(An Important Lesson About Guarding Our Words)

By Dan Corner

Observations From Job's Test

The Job in the Bible was severely tested though he was blameless and upright, an extraordinary man who feared God and shunned evil (1:8).

In other words, Job had wisdom and understanding:

And he said to man, "The fear of the Lord – that is wisdom, and to shun evil is understanding." (Job 28:28)

A wise man fears the LORD and shuns evil, but a fool is hotheaded and reckless. (Prov 14:16)
God's assessment and esteem of Job was very high. He was also a man who persevered a great testing (Jam. 5:11).

So he was tested, but what was Satan's Goal?

But stretch out your hand and strike everything he has, and he will surely curse you to your face. (Job 1:11)

Satan's goal was to get Job to curse God and he tried to accomplish this through Job's wife when she said, "Are you still holding on to your integrity? Curse God and die!" (Job 2:9)

Thankfully, Job rejected her foolish words.

God's Limits On Satan

The LORD said to Satan, "Very well, then, everything he has is in your hands, but on the man himself do not lay a finger." Then Satan went out from the presence of the LORD (Job 1:12).

God placed everything Job had into Satan's hand but prohibited him from laying a finger on Job himself.

The second time God brought Job to Satan's attention, he states:

The LORD said to Satan, "Very well, then, he is in your hands; but you must spare his life." (Job 2:6)

God allowed Satan to painfully afflict Job but assigned a limit on him by commanding that he spare his life.

Job's First Test

After Job's initial bitter tests (1:13–19) of losing his oxen and donkeys, the killing of his servants, the burning up of sheep and servants, the carrying off of his camels, and the destruction of his children, Job states: Naked I came from my mother's womb, and naked I will depart. The LORD gave and the LORD has taken away; may the name of the LORD be praised. (Job 1:21)

In all this, Job did not sin by charging God with wrongdoing (Job 1:22).

Up to this point in his trials, Job does not sin. He's still blameless and upright: Then the LORD said to Satan, "Have you considered my servant Job? There is no one on earth like him; he is blameless and upright, a man who fears God and shuns evil. And he still maintains his integrity, though you incited me against him to ruin him without any reason." (Job 2:3)

Job's Second Test

So Satan went out from the presence of the LORD and afflicted Job with painful sores from the soles of his feet to the top of his head. (Job 2:7)

Remember that God has placed a limit on Satan that he is not to take Job's life. After this painful and severe second test, his wife tempts him to curse God.

Job wisely rebukes her and maintains his integrity. He still hasn't sinned: He replied, "You are talking like a foolish woman. Shall we accept good from God, and not trouble?" In all this, Job did not sin in what he said. (Job 2:10)

God Speaks And Job Repents

After the many discussions between Job and his so-called friends, God speaks to Job out of the storm (38:1–41:34). [This portion of Job is delightful to read as God questions Job and describes his own characteristics.] It is here that Job receives a stiff rebuke from the Lord: Who is this that darkens my counsel with words without knowledge? (Job 38:2) Will the one who contends with the Almighty correct him? Let him who accuses God answer him! (Job 40:2)

Would you discredit my justice? Would you condemn me to justify yourself? (Job 40:8) No one is fierce enough to rouse him. Who then is able to stand against me? (Job 41:10)

Apparently during Job's discussions with his friends, there were occasions when he contended against God, accused him, discredited his justice, condemned God to justify himself, and thought that he could stand against God. After God's rebuke, Job repents:

*My ears had heard of you but now my eyes have seen you. Therefore
I despise myself and repent in dust and ashes. (Job 42:5,6)*

*The devil incited God against Job but could only act within the limits set by
God. In that sense then it was God who brought trouble to Job to test him:*

*All his brothers and sisters and everyone who had known him before
came and ate with him in his house. They comforted and consoled
him over all the trouble the LORD had brought upon him, and
each one gave him a piece of silver and a gold ring. (Job 42:11)*

*Many wonderful passages could be cited of Job's faith and praise
of God. But with all Job's good qualities and that he spoke what
was right about God (42:7,8), in some passages, he apparently
stated things he ought not, was rebuked and had to repent.*

Guard Your Lips

Let this be a powerful lesson to us to guard our lips and watch our words!

*He who guards his lips guards his life, but he who
speaks rashly will come to ruin. (Prov 13:3)
My dear brothers, take note of this: Everyone should be quick to
listen, slow to speak and slow to become angry (James 1:19)
Set a guard over my mouth, O LORD; keep watch
over the door of my lips. (Psa 141:3)
When words are many, sin is not absent, but he who
holds his tongue is wise. (Prov 10:19)*

*If anyone considers himself religious and yet does not keep a tight rein on
his tongue, he deceives himself and his religion is worthless. (James 1:26)*

Remember Job in the bible and how he passed his severe test.
He remembered he was going to be ok. So will you. So will I.

You're Gonna Be Ok
Jenn Johnson

I know it's all you've got to just be strong
And it's a fight just to keep it together
I know you think that you are too far gone
But hope is never lost
Hope is never lost
Hold on, don't let go
Hold on, don't let go
Just take one step closer
Put one foot in front of the other
You'll get through this
Just follow the light in the darkness
You're gonna be ok
I know your heart is heavy from those nights
But just remember that you are a fighter
You never know just what tomorrow holds
And you're stronger than you know
You're stronger than you know
Hold on, don't let go
Hold on, don't let go
Just take one step closer
Put one foot in front of the other
You'll get through this
Just follow the light in the darkness
You're gonna be ok
Just take one step closer
Put one foot in front of the other
You'll get through this
Just follow the light in the darkness
You're gonna be ok
And when the night is closing in
Don't give up and don't give in
This won't last, it's not the end
It's not the end

You're gonna be ok
when the night is closing in
Don't give up and don't give in
This won't last, it's not the end
It's not the end
You're gonna be ok
Songwriter(s): Jenn Johnson; <u>Seth Mosley</u>; Jeremy Riddle
Released: May 8, 2017

"ADONAI bless you and keep you! ADONAI make His face to shine on you and be gracious to you! ADONAI turn His face toward you and grant you shalom!" — Numbers 6:24-26 TLV

'Something Sacred hangs in the balance of every moment' Heschel.

My name is Dr. Shawn Michael Greener and I'm here to tell you, Today is a GREAT day to be ALIVE!

Book of the Bible - Psalms
Author – David, Asaph, the sons of Korah, Solomon, Ethan, Moses, and some are anonymous.
Date of Writing – Between 1440 B.C. and the Babylonian captivity 586 B.C.
Number of Chapters - 150
To Whom Written – Mankind, following the Hebrew people.
Purpose of the Writing – To be music to the ear of God. God is to be worshipped, praised, and confession to God from the depths of our souls is crucial to authentic living.

My Personal Summary–

In our time as <u>*Followers of the Way*</u> in this generation we might be the most-guilty of minimizing obedience and confession in repentance in lieu of over-hyped worship atmospheres that rely upon whipped-up emotion that is *"me focused"* rather than God-directed.

I've been talking about what is authentic and what is hyped for the sake of overhyped whipped up emotionalism.

Psalms reflects *authentic* communication with God, which includes radical praise, prayer and worship along with sincere repentance and confession to God. True Two-way communication…

What is the difference between praise and worship?

Love him or love him not, TD Jakes answers this question perfectly:

> *"Half of the things that pass for worship are not really worship in the church, because if real worship hits the church, the musicians can't play, the ushers can't usher; the Deacons can't be Deacons.*
>
> *It's something that you do out of your belly, out of your heart, out of your spirit.*
>
> *The difference between praise and worship:*
>
> *Anybody can praise God; in fact everybody ought to praise God. Even The bible says let everything that has breath praise the Lord.*
>
> *Anybody can praise God because when you praise God you start praising "Lord I thank You for giving me shoes, I thank You for giving me a suit, I thank You for how You gave me my job, I thank You for how You blessed me with a car, I thank You for how You brought me through college, I thank You for how You helped me in my career.*
>
> *All of that is Praise, praise thanks God for what He already did.*

The praiser is thanking God for his shoes, the worshiper says even if I don't have shoes, even if I don't have car, even if I don't have a home, even if I never get anything, I will worship You for who You are, I worship You because You are God, You don't have to perform, You don't have to impress me, You don't have to play Santa Claus but just because You are God, You mean so much to me, I'll tear up my face and cry, I'll mess up my make-up and cry, ill shag down my hair and cry, oh You are so valuable, your presence is valuable, your love is valuable, your peace is valuable. I just wanna be alone so I can worship you..."

I will grant you, some times, a lot of times we may not FEEL like worshipping and Praising Him... In fact, that is the very last thing we may FEEL like doing! Even If....

*They say sometimes you win some
Sometimes you lose some
And right now, right now I'm losing bad
I've stood on this stage night after night
Reminding the broken it'll be alright
But right now, oh right now I just can't
It's easy to sing
When there's nothing to bring me down
But what will I say
When I'm held to the flame
Like I am right now
I know You're able and I know You can
Save through the fire with Your mighty hand
But even if You don't
My hope is You alone
They say it only takes a little faith
To move a mountain
Well good thing
A little faith is all I have, right now
But God, when You choose*

To leave mountains unmovable
Oh give me the strength to be able to sing
It is well with my soul
I know You're able and I know You can
Save through the fire with Your mighty hand
But even if You don't
My hope is You alone
I know the sorrow, and I know the hurt
Would all go away if You'd just say the word
But even if You don't
My hope is You alone
You've been faithful, You've been good
All of my days
Jesus, I will cling to You
Come what may
'Cause I know You're able
I know You can
I know You're able and I know You can
Save through the fire with Your mighty hand
But even if You don't
My hope is You alone
I know the sorrow, I know the hurt
Would all go away if You'd just say the word
But even if You don't
My hope is You alone
It is well with my soul
It is well, it is well with my soul

Songwriters: Bart Millard / Ben Glover / Crystal
Lewis / David Garcia / Tim Timmons
Even If lyrics © Sony/ATV Music Publishing LLC, Music Services, Inc

I am here to tell you and all the world tonight, that sometimes I do not FEEL like worshipping God… Sometimes pain and dysfunction overwhelm my body… I can't get up, can't sit, and can't stand…. Sometimes I worry if I get on my knees, I won't be able to stand without help…. Then I realize, I remember, Even the Rocks Cry out His Name…. I realize at those moments, there are worse places to get "stuck."

God of creation

There at the start
Before the beginning of time
With no point of reference
You spoke to the dark
And fleshed out the wonder of light
And as You speak
A hundred billion galaxies are born
In the vapor of Your breath the planets form
If the stars were made to worship so will I
I can see Your heart in everything You've made
Every burning star
A signal fire of grace
If creation sings Your praises so will I
God of Your promise
You don't speak in vain
No syllable empty or void
For once You have spoken
All nature and science
Follow the sound of Your voice
And as You speak
A hundred billion creatures catch Your breath
Evolving in pursuit of what You said
If it all reveals Your nature so will I
I can see Your heart in everything You say
Every painted sky
A canvas of Your grace
If creation still obeys You so will I
So will I
So will I
If the stars were made to worship so will I

If the mountains bow in reverence so will I
If the oceans roar Your greatness so will I
For if everything exists to lift You high so will I
If the wind goes where You send it so will I
If the rocks cry out in silence so will I
If the sum of all our praises still falls shy
Then we'll sing again a hundred billion times
God of salvation
You chased down my heart
Through all of my failure and pride
On a hill You created
The light of the world
Abandoned in darkness to die
And as You speak
A hundred billion failures disappear
Where You lost Your life so I could find it here
If You left the grave behind You so will I
I can see Your heart in everything You've done
Every part designed in a work of art called love
If You gladly chose surrender so will I
I can see Your heart
Eight billion different ways
Every precious one
A child You died to save
If You gave Your life to love them so will I
Like You would again a hundred billion times
But what measure could amount to Your desire
You're the One who never leaves the one behind

Songwriters: Joel Houston / Benjamin Hastings / Michael Fatkin
So Will I (100 Billion X) lyrics © Capitol Christian Music Group

The Book of Psalms accounts for times when believers were deeply sorrowful and hurting greatly in their lives, and they expressed that sorrow to God.

Exactly when we need to praise God the most, the deepest, the most authentically, that is exactly when we are hurting the deepest, the hardest....

The most hopeless times. THEN is when our praise and worship needs to be the deepest.... What a conundrum right?

Those who doubted and feared expressed that doubt and fear to/of/ for God.

In the same vigor, true believers worshipped God in an incredibly authentic way. They weren't concerned with being hip, trendy and cool; rather, they were authentic and unrestrained because they revered God, knowing He knows them.

In the process of this authentic praise, worship, and repentance, the people asked God for help in times of real need, though with reverence.

Psalms 56:8-13 might be one of my favorite passages of the Bible in that I am reminded that as God heard the Psalmist, so too He hears me.

We matter to Him...
We matter to God....
He feels our sorrows, as we cannot imagine...

> Psalms 56:8-13 (NASB) *Ps 56:8 You have taken account of my wanderings; Put my tears in Your bottle. Are they not in Your book? 9 Then my enemies will turn back in the day when I call; This I know, that God is for me. 10In God, whose word I praise, In the Lord, whose word I praise, 11 In God I have put my trust, I shall not be afraid. What can man do to me? 12 Your vows are binding upon me, O God; I will render thank offerings to You. 13 For You have delivered my (1)soul from death, Indeed my (2)feet from stumbling, So that I may (3)walk before God In the light of the living.*

Psalms convicts me that I am not praising and worshipping God deeply enough, authentically enough, often enough so as to forget about my inhibitions and self-consciousness enough.

Psalms also convicts me that I am not repenting deeply enough so as to forget my pride and self-reliance.

In many respects, I can say I've worried about "*letting go*" in my worship and praise to be fully present with God…. People worry about looking a certain 'respectable' way, during worship and praise… We want to look "*reserved*" "*respectful*" "*righteous.*" We want to look, "*in control.*"

I have to ask, Why is it we are so concerned with appearing "*in control in front of people who do not hold our destiny and our eternity in their hands!?*"

The truth revealed to me in reading the Psalms is that I am far more sinful than I think and God is far greater than I realize and in the end I am to repent to Him and Worship Him, from now until the end of my days when I will meet Him in person. I can only imagine, what will I do then?

I Can Only Imagine
Mercy Me

I can only imagine what it will be like
When I walk, by your side
I can only imagine what my eyes will see
When you face is before me
I can only imagine
I can only imagine
Surrounded by You glory
What will my heart feel
Will I dance for you Jesus

Or in awe of You be still
Will I stand in your presence
Or to my knees will I fall
Will I sing hallelujah
Will I be able to speak at all
I can only imagine
I can only imagine
I can only imagine when that day comes
When I find myself standing in the Son
I can only imagine when all I would do is forever
Forever worship You
I can only imagine
I can only imagine
Surrounded by Your glory
What will my heart feel
Will I dance for You, Jesus
Or in awe of you be still
Will I stand in your presence
Or to my knees will I fall
Will I sing hallelujah
Will I be able to speak at all
I can only imagine
I can only imagine hey ya ah
Surrounded by Your glory
What will my heart feel
Will I dance for You, Jesus
Or in awe of you be still
Will I stand in Your presence
Or to my knees will I fall
Will I sing hallelujah
Will I be able to speak at all
I can only imagine
I can only imagine hey ya ah
I can only imagine yeah yeah
I can only imagine

I can only imagine ey ey ey
I can only imagine
I can only imagine when all I will do
Is forever, forever worship You
I can only imagine

Songwriters: Bart Marshall Millard

If you acquire nothing else from this summary of this great book of the Bible, please take this to heart... The Book of Psalms starts and ends with praise. Worship and Praise at the beginning and the end, inside and out. The passage speaks to me that I must be captured to be free. My friend, life begins with praise. Life ends with praise. The 'in between" determines the intensity of our final praise here on earth, before we begin our eternal praise with God in Heaven.

Psalm 150 Tree of Life Version (TLV)

Praise with **Shofar** and Cymbals

Psalm 150

¹ Halleluyah! Praise God in His Sanctuary!
Praise Him in His mighty expanse.

² Praise Him for His acts of power.
Praise Him for His enormous greatness.

³ Praise Him with the blast of the shofar.
Praise Him with harp and lyre.

⁴ Praise Him with tambourine and dance.
Praise Him with string instruments and flute.

⁵ Praise Him with clash of cymbals.
Praise Him with resounding cymbals.

> [6] *Let everything that has breath*
> *praise Adonai. Halleluyah!*

Tree of Life Version (TLV)

Tree of Life (TLV) Translation of the Bible. Copyright © 2015
by The Messianic Jewish Family Bible Society.

Book of the Bible - Proverbs
Author – Solomon, Agur and Lemuel
Date of Writing – 971 – 931 B.C.
Number of Chapters - 31
To Whom Written – The young Israelites near the wisest mortal man
to ever live, Solomon.
Purpose of the Writing – To bring about wisdom paths to the youth,
and the mature that would listen to wisdom, and the leader who might
not know it all…

My Personal Summary–

Even though Solomon is billed as the wisest man on Earth, he failed
often.

When someone as wealthy as Solomon fails that is a Texas Sized heads
up to us that there are lessons to be learned if only the reader will take
advantage of the experiences of others. We are blessed beyond measure
to have the words and thoughts of Solomon written in such an easy to
follow medium as the Book of Proverbs.

> *Proverbs 1:1-7 (NASB)* [Pr 1:1] *The proverbs of Solomon the son of
> David, king of Israel:* [2] *To know wisdom and instruction, To
> discern the sayings of understanding,* [3] *To receive instruction
> in wise behavior, Righteousness, justice and equity;* [4] *To
> give prudence to the naive, To the youth knowledge and
> discretion,* [5] *A wise man will hear and increase in learning,
> And a man of understanding will acquire wise counsel,* [6] *To
> understand a proverb and a figure, The words of the wise*

*and their riddles. ⁷ The fear of the Lord is the beginning of
knowledge; Fools despise wisdom and instruction.*

Or,
Proverbs 21:19
*19 It is better to live in a desert land than with a quarrelsome,
worrisome wife.*

(See, if I was already wise and didn't need wisdom, I would have left
verse 19 off.. Seeing as I have to ride home with my wife from my radio
broadcasts... over a tall bridge.. See? Wisdom a verse at a time! Pray for
me to make it home!)

*20 Precious treasure and oil are in a wise person's dwelling,
but a foolish person devours all he has.
21 Whoever pursues righteousness and mercy
finds life, prosperity, and honor.
22 A wise person scales the city of warriors
and brings down the stronghold in which they trust.
23 Whoever guards his mouth and tongue
keeps his soul out of troubles.
24 A proud and haughty man
—Mocker is his name—
acts with overbearing pride.
25 A slacker's craving will kill him,
because his hands refuse to work.
26 All day long he craves greedily,
yet the righteous one gives and does not hold back.*

After leading us on a path that surely includes whatever station of life
any reader may occupy, for the young person, the naïve, the wise man,
and a man of understanding we are given in Chapter 1, Verse 7; the key,
the utter link to any pursuit and acquisition of wisdom; *"fear of the Lord."*

This is followed precipitously by the rebuke of fools who identify
themselves by despising wisdom and instruction. Sometimes I am a
fool. If we all are being honest, many of us are... fools.

God directed Solomon to include these chapters from a collection of his <u>3,000</u> proverbs leading me to believe these are the most salient and relevant, not only for the audience of Solomon's time, but also for my generation.

We are not relegated to sail in this dangerous and complex Ocean helplessly rudderless for the simplest or most complex storms we face in life.

God gave us these Proverbs from which we receive amazing tidbits of instruction from Solomon's vast experience. Proverbs isn't just a Book of the Bible, it is an instruction manual…. For Life.

How do we live a wise life in light of the snare's present in this dangerous and conflict filled world?

I will give you the how….

When we aren't busy praising and worshipping God with reckless abandon, like only God is looking… We read and study Proverbs!

Proverbs is presumed to be the book of Solomon's middle-aged years with the knowledge that Solomon had already experienced in a litany of challenges that frankly, you or I will likely face.

"ADONAI bless you and keep you! ADONAI make His face to shine on you and be gracious to you! ADONAI turn His face toward you and grant you shalom!" — Numbers 6:24-26 TLV

'Something Sacred hangs in the balance of every moment' Heschel.

My name is Dr. Shawn Michael Greener and I'm here to tell you, Today is a GREAT day to be ALIVE!

- *The valley of Achor for a door of hope,* <u>*Hosea 2:15*</u>. *See* <u>*Joshua 7:24-26*</u>.
- *"Joined to idols,"* <u>*Hosea 4:17*</u>.
- *"Mixes... with the nations" (no longer a separated and holy nation),* <u>*Hosea 7:8*</u>.
- *"A cake not turned" (dough on one side, expressing half-heartedness),* <u>*Hosea 7:8*</u>.
- *Strangers devour his strength" (weakened by evil associations),* <u>*Hosea 7:9*</u>.
- *"Grey hairs also are sprinkled on him" (premature old age and unconscious deterioration),* <u>*Hosea 7:9*</u>.
- *"Israel swallowed up" (national identity lost),* <u>*Hosea 8:8*</u>.
- *"A vessel in which no one delights" (a marred and useless vessel to the Lord),* <u>*Hosea 8:8*</u>.
- *"False balances" (commercial trickery in business),* <u>*Hosea 12:7*</u>.

Given the previous nine instances of imagery addressing real world challenges, one cannot deny the relevance of God's Word to modern challenges.

Book of the Bible - Joel
Author – Joel, which means in Hebrew, *"Jehovah is God."*
Date of Writing – Unclear
Number of Chapters – 3
To Whom Written – Southern Kingdom of Judah
Purpose of the Writing – Joel serves as a warning to the people of Judah of God's impending judgment because of their sins.

My Personal Summary–

As in Daniel 9 a pleading prayer was offered to God for His disobedient people by the prophet Joel offered soul deep pleading for the change in Judah. A plague of locusts is sent by God to discipline His disobedient people devastating the foliage in Judah. God issued this discipline, and a severe drought as a direct result of the sins of the people. As in Daniel 9 Joel rings the clarion for national repentance, but it goes unheeded.

A promise of deliverance was made conditional upon the people of Judah turning from their sins which led to the oft-quoted verse Joel 2:25:

Joel 2:25 (NASB)

Joel 2:25 *"Then I will make up to you for the years That the swarming locust has eaten, The creeping locust, the stripping locust and the gnawing locust, My great army which I sent among you.*

We are taught an underlying lesson in this passage; God can and will use all of this world, including animals present in nature to effect His judgment which further illustrations God's sovereignty over His entire creation.

Joel 2:28-32 (NASB)

Joel 2:28 *"It will come about after this That I will pour out My Spirit on all mankind; And your sons and daughters will prophesy, Your old men will dream dreams, Your young men will see visions.*

29 *"Even on the male and female servants I will pour out My Spirit in those days.*

30 *"I will display wonders in the sky and on the earth, Blood, fire and columns of smoke.*

31 *"The sun will be turned into darkness and the moon into blood Before the great and awesome day of the Lord comes.*

32 *"And it will come about that whoever calls on the name of the Lord Will be delivered; For on Mount Zion and in Jerusalem There will be those who escape, As the Lord has said, Even among the survivors whom the Lord calls.*

There are many benefits to obedience to God, not the least of which is an escape of punishment. As we see in the above passage, another benefit of obedience is the revelation of the Holy Spirit in our lives, which amplifies the learned assertion that without obedience there can be no indwelling of the Holy Spirit.

Without the Holy Spirit of the Living God no people, no matter how "chosen" will prosper. This indwelling comes only to the obedient believer.

Book of the Bible – Amos, which means "Burden Bearer" in Hebrew.
Author – Amos
Date of Writing – 755-750 B.C.
Number of Chapters – 9
To Whom Written – The Northern Kingdom, Israel.
Purpose of the Writing – To pronounce God's just judgment on His sinful people

My Personal Summary–

Amos is unique because he was poor herdsman in Judah; however he traveled to where the rich spent their leisure time to tell them of their iniquities and the price to be paid for disobedience of God. Amos spoke mostly against the social and economic sins of Israel while he, a poor man caring for poor man's fruit was answering the call of God, without question.

We understand clearly from Amos' ministry that caring for the poor and disadvantaged is an important mission of Christ-followers, far more so than to build expansive church buildings and softball and basketball leagues and afternoon tea clubs. Today the "great" churches need to be aware of the motivation to provide new programs that do not address the social needs of their communities while they do provide recreation for those already blessed. Amos knew then what we should know now, we do not need another church basketball league while hundreds of children in a five mile radius from their church have no winter coats in the bitter cold.

Amos was very clear to the people of his time and following that judgment is coming and it was a judgment of fire upon a sinful people. We, in America could well-deed that same warning today. Many of the people of our country have many opulent homes while many of the poor have no place to call home. Materialism is not a new sin, Amos called us out in 755 B.C. and we still have not learned.

Book of the Bible – Obadiah, which means "Servant of the Lord."
Author – Probably Obadiah
Date of Writing – Uncertain, possibly 605-586 B.C.
Number of Chapters – 1
To Whom Written – The Edomites and God's people.
Purpose of the Writing – God's faithfulness to His people would be revealed in the devastation of Edom for being so cruel to Judah. This book is the account of that declaration.

My Personal Summary–

Very little that happens in the Bible is unrelated at least some way. This is certainly the case with Obadiah in that rifts between Esau and Jacob over red stew and refused passage to the Promised Land.

Edom would be destroyed because of their debauchery and misplaced pride over the demise of Israel at the hands of other countries while Edom sat silently by, allowing their brother to fall then to gloat about it.

Edom thought it would be secure because of its mountain outposts and the Edomites flouted their perceived security before a Holy God and they would systematically fall to Israel as Israel prospered greatly and Edom fell into obscurity.

Edom's pride would fall, their wealth eliminated, and their people killed but what concisely did they do to bring this upon themselves? They were arrogant, disloyal, and violent toward their "brother" Israel. Yes, it was that simple! Ultimately we are all reminded to be loyal, faithful, and humble lest we fall as Edom fell.

Edom's demise reveals judgment to come against any nation who mistreats Israel though we know God punishes in accordance to their violations against Him, we also know the punishment is severe. Edom was a traitor to Israel and they celebrated Israel's losses by drinking and dancing and yet that joyful laughter would turn to death and tears because our God is just. Israel is restored at God's command as Edom falls.

"The Lord has spoken "and thus, what is prophesied will come to pass.

Book of the Bible - Jonah
Author – Jonah, son of Amittai
Date of Writing – Between 783 B.C. and 753 B.C.
Number of Chapters – 4 only four.
To Whom Written – Israel and all people to follow
Purpose of the Writing – Only God can bring salvation to anyone who repents of their sins and return to Him.

My Personal Summary–

Jonah is much like me initially when God called me into the ministry; I did not want to go either. Jonah hated the Ninevites and did not want to go to them because of his hatred for the very people to whom he called to minister. Lest you think my similarity to Jonah is that I hate my audience and congregation… that is most assuredly not the case. I love my audience and congregation. No, the issue is that I most often don't fancy myself as a suitable minister of the gospel. You see, I know all of my hurts habits and hang-ups and if I were to choose someone to preach my gospel, it wouldn't be me. I wouldn't call me.

Ultimately the mission we are called to is the will of God for our lives. If we do not comply, God will get our attention the easy way or the hard way. Jonah chose the hard way, which involved a big fish. Who cares if it was a whale, or some other species? What actually matters is this; God will use whatever means necessary to either gain compliance or we will swim with the sharks of disobedience and judgment.

When we are disobedient to God, the other people in the boat that is our lives will surely cast us out because the storm that God often sends to get our attention throws waves in the laps of those that have to watch the penalty come upon us from a Holy God.

Eventually Jonah, "the Popular Prophet" reluctantly obeyed God and in so doing, Jonah gave the give of salvation knowledge and in addition to coming into compliance, they also came into God's blessings and favor. Jonah wanted to die because God showed His favor upon the repentant people of Nineveh. Jonah would rather die than to have God's mercy shown upon the people of ancient Mosul, Iraq. God gave the retreating Jonah shade for his head and God's lessons are perfect and in that perfection Jonah learned that God is indeed perfect and compassionate, even though we are not. God is a God of second chances.

You might take a look at the end of the Book of Jonah. It won't take you long to get there because there are only four chapters.

> Jonah 4:2-4 Tree of Life Version (TLV)
> *² So he prayed to Adonai* and said, "Please, Lord, was not this what I said when I was still in my own country? That's what I anticipated, fleeing to Tarshish—for I knew that you are a gracious and compassionate God, **slow to anger and _full_ of kindness**, *and relenting over calamity. ³ So please, Adonai, take my soul from me—because better is my death than my life."*
>
> *⁴ Yet Adonai* said, "Is it good for you to be so angry?"

Tree of Life Version (TLV)
Tree of Life (TLV) Translation of the Bible. Copyright © 2015 by The Messianic Jewish Family Bible Society.

Jonah would rather **D I E** than to have the people, who heard the message God told Jonah to deliver, and they LISTENED and heeded the message! Yet, Jonah would rather they be burnt up in God's wrath than to be saved by turning around and obeying God's commands. Jonah was not unlike many of us where we want people to "pay" rather than to change their path and receive mercy and salvation.

I heard a pastor say once, and I believe he was quoting another pastor, *"The consequences of a calloused heart is a complaining mouth."* Philippians 2:14,15 highlights a very important point…

> Philippians 2:14-16 Tree of Life Version (TLV)
> *14 Do everything without grumbling or arguing, 15 so that you might be blameless and innocent, children of God in the midst of a crooked and twisted generation. Among them you shine as lights in the world, 16 holding fast to the word of life, so that I may boast in the day of Messiah that I did not run or labor in vain.*

Tree of Life Version (TLV)
Tree of Life (TLV) Translation of the Bible. Copyright © 2015 by The Messianic Jewish Family Bible Society.

Without grumbling or arguing? **EVERYTHING?** Often Christians cannot do ONE thing without grumbling or arguing! I am guilty too! Look at the tail end of verse 15. *Among them **you shine** as lights in the world…* Sometimes I feel like a 15 watt LED light… dim as all get out.

I have heard it said, *"Everyone likes being viewed as a servant until they get treated like one."* I've also heard it said, usually I say it when people express sympathy at me being terminally ill…. *"Everyone wants to go to Heaven but nobody wants to die!"* Jonah makes me think that perhaps more people in this modern natural world would come to Christ if we actually didn't think somehow *"they have Hell coming to them."* This is tantamount to the folks that find a super great quiet country place on farmland near the woods and ocean and mountains and as soon as the last nail gets driven into the home they want all development to stop. I got MY house; you build yours somewhere NOT here!

I got MY salvation and redemption… You get yours some other way. But, there is no other way. It cracks me up and convicts me at the same time how Jonah so suddenly ends. God ends the Book of Jonah abruptly, but very much worth pondering.

> *9Then God said to Jonah, "Is it good for you to be so angry about the plant?" "It is," he said, "I am angry enough to die!"*
>
> *10But Adonai* said, "You have pity on the plant for which you did no labor or make it grow, that appeared overnight and perished overnight. So shouldn't I have pity on Nineveh— the great city that has in it more than 120,000 people who don't know their right hand from their left—as well as many animals?"

Copyright © 2014 - Messianic Jewish Family Bible Society

God specifically identifies the animals as worth protecting and I support that!

Book of the Bible - Micah
Author – Micah
Date of Writing – 739-686 B.C.
Number of Chapters – 7
To Whom Written – Israel and Judah
Purpose of the Writing – The warning of God's judgment for the sinful people and the echo of the mercy of God.

My Personal Summary–

Social justice in Israel and Judah was heavily on Micah's mind as he preached of a coming judgment because of the "Have's" taking advantage of the "Have-not's." I see thirteen close comparisons of verses in Micah with verses in Isaiah, which tells me and the literate world that there is a divine cohesiveness in the Word of God.

The Pharisee's that killed Yeshua killed Him because He didn't observe the Hebrew customs as they thought He should. They killed Him because He threatened their status quo and their power base. Micah speaks to this culture as people valued material possessions more than their spiritual condition. These same people oppressed those who were less fortunate from a place of undeserved piety.

The people of Judah carefully observed the orthodoxy of their faith but their hearts were deaf to the Spirit of God. Their practice was clean however their hearts were dirty and Micah saw this and was not swayed by their rituals because Micah had a deeper vision of the people based on the observation that the people of Judah were unjust and dispassionate to those they oppressed.

Doctrinally we may be correct, but in the practice of our faith, the demonstration of our transformation if we are devoid of compassion and justice then our practice is wasted and disingenuous.

God offers hope to the people Judah and in that hope those of my generation have hope because we too are venturing far from our faith and practice.

Book of the Bible - Nahum
Author – Nahum – "Compassionate" "Full of comfort."
Date of Writing – Between 612 b.c. – 664 b.c.
Number of Chapters - 3
To Whom Written – The people of Judah and the citizens of Nineveh
Purpose of the Writing – To foretell of God's judgment is coming as vengeance for the Ninevites and God promises deliverance for the people of Judah.

My Personal Summary–

Sovereignty is a concept not readily assimilated in modern society, yet when we speak of God, Sovereignty is a critical component we need to understand in order to properly worship and serve God. Nahum truly amplifies the sovereignty of God because in Nahum's prophetic revelation of God's impending judgment upon the people of Nineveh God displayed His love for His people because He cared enough to discipline them.

God is fully in control of history and He loves His people enough to discipline them and this speaks of His sovereignty in that His people that are obedient can rest assured that God will take care of those that are disobedient, in His time and way.

The frenetic and wild attack on Nineveh is unmistakably graphic however it reminds us that when God renders punishment upon the disobedient it clears the way for God's obedient people to be released from their poor conditions, but in God's time and in His way.

There were twelve prophecies that Nahum gave that we can confirm were fulfilled. They are: (Walvoord 1985)

> *Nahum's Prophecies*
> *Historical Fulfillments[3]*
>
> *1. The Assyrian fortresses surrounding the city would be easily captured (3:12).*
>
> *1. According to the Babylonian Chronicle the fortified towns in Nineveh's environs began to fall in 614 B.C. including Tabris, present–day Sharif Khan, a few miles northwest of Nineveh.*

---

[3] Elliott E. Johnson, *The Bible Knowledge Commentary: An Exposition of the Scriptures by Dallas Seminary Faculty*, ed. John Walvoord and Roy Zuck (Colorado Springs, CO: Cook Communications, 1985), WORDsearch CROSS e-book, 1496.

2. The besieged Ninevites would prepare bricks and mortar for emergency defense walls (3:14).

2. A. T. Olmstead reported: "To the south of the gate, the moat is still filled with fragments of stone and mud bricks from the walls, heaped up when they were breached" History of Assyria, Chicago: University of Chicago Press, 1951, p. 637).

3. The city gates would be destroyed (3:13).

3. Olmstead noted: "The main attack was directed from the northwest and the brunt fell upon the Hatami gate at this corner... While the gate are traces of the counter wall raised by the inhabitants in their last extremity" (History of Assyria, p. 637).

4. In the final hours of the attack the Ninevites would be drunk (1:10; 3:11).

4. Diodorus Siculus (ca. 20 B.C.) wrote, "The Assyrian king... distributed to his soldiers meats and liberals supplies of wine and provisions... While the whole army was thus carousing, the friends of Arbakes learned from some deserters of the slackness and drunkenness which prevailed in the enemy's camp and made an unexpected attack by night" (Bibliotheca Historica 2. 26. 4)

5. Nineveh would be destroyed by a flood (1:8; 2:6, 8)

5. Diodorus wrote that in the third year of the siege heavy rains caused a nearby river to flood part of the walls (Bibliotheca Historica 2. 26. 9; 2. 27. 13). Xenophon referred to terrifying thunder (presumably with a storm) associated with the city's capture (Anabasis, 3. 14. 12). Also the Khosr River, entering the city from the northwest at the Ninlil Gate and running through the city in a southwesterly

direction, may have flooded because of heavy rains, or the enemy may have destroyed its sluice gate.

6. Nineveh would be destroyed by fire (<u>1:10</u>; <u>2:13</u>; <u>3:15</u>)

6. Archeological excavations at Nineveh revealed charred wood, charcoal, and ashes. "There was no question about the clear traces of the burning of the temple (as also in the palace of Sennacherib), for a layer of ash about two inches thick lay clearly defined in the places on the southeast side about the level of the Sargon pavement" (R. Campbell Thompson and R.W. Hutchinson, A Century of Exploration at Nineveh, London: Luzac, 1929, pp. 45, 77).

7. The city's capture would be attended by a great massacre of people. (<u>3:3</u>)

7. "In two battles fought on the plain before the city the rebels defeated the Assyrians... So great was the multitude of the slain that following a stream, mingled with their blood, changed its color for a considerable distance" (Diodorus, Bibliotheca Historica, 2. 26. 6-7).

8. Plundering and pillaging would accompany the overthrow of the city (<u>2:9-10</u>)

8. According the Babylonian Chronicle, "Great quantities of the spoil of the city, beyond counting, they carried it off. The city [they turned] into a mound and ruin heap" (Luckenbill, Ancient Records of Assyria and Babylonia, 2:420).

9. When Nineveh would be captured its people would try to escape (<u>2:8</u>).

9. "Sardanapalus [another name for King Sin-shar-ishkun] went away his three sons and two daughters with much treasure into Paphlagonia, to the governor of Kattos, the most loyal of his subjects" (Diodorus, Bibliotheca Historica, 2. 26. 8).

10. The Ninevite officers would weaken and flee (3:17).

10. The Babylonian Chronicle states that "[The army] of Assyria deserted [lit., ran away before] the king" Luckenbill, Ancient Records of Assyria and Babylonia, 2:420)

11. Nineveh's images and idols would be destroyed (1:14).

11. Campbell Thompson and R.W. Hutchinson reported that the statue of the goddess Ishtar lay headless in the debris of Nineveh's ruins ("The British Museum Excavations on the Temple of Ishtar at Nineveh, 1930-1," Annals of Archeology and Anthropology. 19, pp. 55-6)

12. Nineveh's destruction would be final (1:9, 14).

12. Many cities of the ancient Near East were rebuilt after being destroyed (e.g., Samaria, Jerusalem, Babylon) but not Nineveh.

What God says He will do, He does. Based on Nahum and several other Biblical books, we cannot claim we were not told.

Book of the Bible - Habakkuk
Author – Possibly Habakkuk
Date of Writing – Possibly between 609 B.C. and 597 B.C.
Number of Chapters – 3
To Whom Written – Judah and God's people asking difficult life-questions.
Purpose of the Writing – To remind Habakkuk and those listening to him that God is the one true God who is in complete control and can be completely trusted.

My Personal Summary–

Wrestling with God is a low profit activity. It has been said that "Our arms are too short to box with God." Ultimately Habakkuk said what most of us are too afraid to say when something terrible happens; "How could you do this God!" "How long will you let this go on?" "Why did you let this happen?" The book of Habakkuk was intended for the eyes of Israel because of the godly peoples wondering when the oppression, wickedness in Judah was happening to them and there seemed to be no help from God. God seemed silent until He enacted evil Babylon in His plan to punish Judah. God answered and yet the Israelites could not understand why God would use an evil people to punish Judah. That is understandable, but in the end, God uses whatever He wants to affect His will.

God would punish the Babylonians in His time, in His way. I am often impatient as to God's will be done. More often than not, I am the benefactor of His delay. His grace and mercy envelops me despite my deserving punishment. The trick is, as is revealed in this book of the Bible, is to be patient and know that He is God and He will take care of things, in His way, in His time. The real trick is, to worship Him while we wait.

If you are feeling oppressed, be obedient, God will take care of you, in His way, in His time.

Book of the Bible - Zephaniah
Author - Zephaniah
Date of Writing – Shortly before 628 B.C.
Number of Chapters – 3
To Whom Written – Judah and surrounding nations
Purpose of the Writing – To further motivate God's people to repent and return to God.

My Personal Summary–

The past several books of the Bible have been that of a warning of God's judgment should the people not repent, the nations turn collectively to God and to turn from their idols. Zephaniah was part of the reminders to the people of Judah who comprised a syncretistic "Shameful Nation."

Zephaniah was not issuing a warning just for the people of God; he was also issuing a warning for the pagan nations surrounding Judah. Ultimately as detailed in verse 3 in chapter 2 those who were serving God were challenged to serve continually because God would provide them protection from His judgment.

However, as Ammon and Moab would soon learn, as descendants of Lot, they face greater judgment for their offenses. In many respects, "They should have known better." So should I.

The foretelling of Nineveh's fall and the utter decimation of Assyria was given in verse 13 and in only twenty years after the prophetic words were spoken, Nineveh fell. The long-range prophecy had to deal with a great war of the nations and their destruction under the fierce anger of God. "Pride would indeed go before their fall." The remaining people will be a meek and truthful people of God who do good in His Name.

Zephaniah concludes with the repeated promise from God that God will one day gather His people and restore to them great fortunes. Interestingly, Zephaniah indicted both the religious and civil leaders of Jerusalem for their oppression and arrogance in order to fill their pockets with loot.

Book of the Bible - Haggai

Author –Haggai, "The Prophet of the Temple."

Date of Writing – 520 B.C.

Number of Chapters - 2

To Whom Written – The Remnant, those returning from Exile in Babylon

Purpose of the Writing – To announce the blessings of God would not return until they placed God first, finished the temple, and restored God-honoring worship.

My Personal Summary–

When I think of the emphasis we place upon our homes, the appearance, the amenities, the location, I cannot help but wonder why the church has taken such a back-seat to our mortal residences? As the Remnant returned they found God's house in ruins and as the people were busy rebuilding their dream homes they failed to give due attention to the House of the Holy God to whom they owed all. God would use the prophet Haggai to speak to their selfishness and their disobedience with specificity unlike any other at that time.

Where God reproofs He gives opportunity for encouragement in the presence of obedience. All the while, despite some great effort, the temple they completed paled in comparison to that of Solomon's both in size and splendor. Haggai told of a new indwelling of the Messiah, coming in great divine power completely filling the house of God.

When I compare my home to many churches I see evidence of people giving their last, left-over fruits in lieu of their first fruits, as is commanded. This comes from a shoddy attempt to placate God with half-hearted obedience as thought the most sovereign God could be placated by anything we could do, for we are not holy or worthy of God.

God protects and loves His children and those who are obedient will be secure in the knowledge of promise that God fight our battles, vanquish our foes, and restore us in His mercy. Obedience is key!

Book of the Bible - Zechariah
Author - Zechariah
Date of Writing – 520-519 B.C.
Number of Chapters - 14
To Whom Written – The Remnant
Purpose of the Writing – To bring hope to God's people during tough times while encouraging spiritual revival to turn their collective hearts back to the Lord.

My Personal Summary–

In one night Zechariah saw eight dynamic visions, which were interpreted by an angel. The visions and meanings were:

Zechariah's Eight Night Visions
Vision
Reference
Meaning[4]

The Red-horse Rider among the Myrtles
1:7-17
God's anger against the nations and blessing on restored Israel
The Four Horns and the Four Craftsmen
1:18-21
God's judgment on the nations that afflict Israel
The Surveyor with a Measuring Line
Chapter 2
God's future blessing on restored Israel
The Cleansing and Crowning of Joshua the High Priest
Chapter 3
Israel's future cleansing from sin and reinstatement as a priestly nation
The Golden Lamp stand and Two Olive Trees

---

[4] John Walvoord and Roy Zuck, ed., *The Bible Knowledge Commentary: An Exposition of the Scriptures by Dallas Seminary Faculty,* (Colorado Springs, CO: Cook Communications, 1985), WORD*search* CROSS e-book, 1549.

Chapter 4
Israel as the light to the nations under Messiah, the King-Priest
The Flying Scroll
<u>5:1-4</u>
The severity and totality of divine judgment on individual Israelites
The Woman in the Ephah
<u>5:5-11</u>
The removal of national Israel's sin of rebellion against God
The Four Chariots
<u>6:1-5</u>
Divine judgment on Gentile nations

> ### Zechariah 9:9 (NASB)
> *Rejoice greatly, O daughter of Zion! Shout in triumph, O daughter of Jerusalem! Behold, your king is coming to you; He is just and endowed with salvation, Humble, and mounted on a donkey, Even on a colt, the foal of a donkey.*

The Messiah is foretold! The Lord God is sending a King! Yeshua is coming humbly, full of justice and salvation and He is coming to me! Solo Deo Gloria! I remember the first time I read this verse and realized what it was say was when I was five years old and it stopped me in my little tracks because it meant I had hope and hope was foretold. In other words, I could trust it.

Then I read the following passage and I understood that the prophecy was not just for the Messiah's life, but also His death. I remember being devastated that the story of my redemption was so quickly told.

> ### Zechariah 12:10-11 (NASB)
> Zec 12:10 *"I will pour out on the house of David and on the inhabitants of Jerusalem, the Spirit of grace and of supplication, so that they will look on Me whom they have pierced; and they will mourn for Him, as one mourns for an only son, and they will weep bitterly over Him like the bitter weeping over a firstborn.*

¹¹ "In that day there will be great mourning in Jerusalem, like the mourning of Hadadrimmon in the plain of Megiddo.

Zechariah looked toward the coming glory and that glory would come at the Hand of the coming Messiah, Yeshua. Zechariah was often called the Prophet of the Long Vision because his prophesy looked quite far into the future, even as in the prophetic statement above, that the Messiah would come from the house of David and that He would be pierced and that He would be an only Son.

I find chapters 7 and 8 particularly interesting in that the people are called out for their insincerity in their fasting and other observances, as the Apostles would also do in the New Testament. When I parallel that revelation with the realization that the Jewish Nation will one day deeply regret their killing and rejection of their Messiah, I wonder who could ever doubt the authenticity of the Holy Bible.

Book of the Bible - Malachi
Author - Malachi
Date of Writing – 430 B.C.
Number of Chapters – 4
To Whom Written – Jerusalem and their sinful leaders
Purpose of the Writing – Yet another warning to God's people and their leaders to obey and return to God because without holiness, the righteous and the wicked will be judged.

My Personal Summary–

Malachi 1:1-5 (NASB)
Mal 1:1 *The oracle of the word of the Lord to Israel through Malachi.*

² "I have loved you," says the Lord. But you say, "How have You loved us?" "Was not Esau Jacob's brother?" declares the Lord. "Yet I have loved Jacob;

³ but I have hated Esau, and I have made his mountains a desolation and appointed his inheritance for the jackals of the wilderness."

⁴ Though Edom says, "We have been beaten down, but we will return and build up the ruins"; thus says the Lord of hosts, "They may build, but I will tear down; and men will call them the wicked territory, and the people toward whom the Lord is indignant forever."

⁵ Your eyes will see this and you will say, "The Lord be magnified beyond the border of Israel!"

What amazing words to hear from the prophet Malachi! Ultimately, God is sovereign, totally and completely sovereign. The people had been bringing second-hand offerings and their tithes were insignificant and not from the right heart, and thus, not sufficient for a Holy God.

The priests failed in training the people regarding God's law. Divorce was seen as a way of life and the priests were not preaching against it. Corruption was seen as a way of life. Withholding from God was seen as a way of life, and the priests were silent and complicit. It is not much different today. *"Prosperity Preachers"* intentionally distort the Word to suit their own agendas, and they subject themselves to God's intense punishment.

The practice of calling evil good was not foreign to the Malachi's audience. Even today pornographic movies are labeled "mature." Abortion advocates are called "pro-choice." People who disagree with the practice of homosexuality are called "intolerant." Our entire language is nuanced such that even in politics, when someone gets caught cheating on their spouse claims they made a "mistake." Our vernacular is co-opted to lower the banner of holiness into the mud of self-indulgence. This is what was happening to Malachi's audience, and to my generation. The Refiner's fire is coming and His fire will purify all, including me.

John the Baptist was prophesied to come, who would then prophesy the coming of Yeshua, our Savior. The Old and New Testament are knitted perfectly together in this amazing book of Malachi. Thank God we have hope!

THE NEW TESTAMENT – B'RIT CHADASHAH

Book of the Bible – Matthew
Author - Matthew (also called Levi)
Date of Writing – A.D. 60
Number of Chapters - 28
To Whom Written – The Jews
Purpose of the Writing – To establish that Yeshua of Nazareth was the prophesied Messiah.

My Personal Summary–

Yeshua is here! He and our salvation are upon us! Hope and help are come so that we might be released from animal sacrifice and from the penalty we deserve. It is astounding to me that God sent His Son in the form of a baby, in lieu of any other form He could have chosen. A baby, just as we enter the world, Yeshua entered the world.

In the beginning of Matthew we are given the genealogy of the King, which to many is boring, and to some extent, felt by some, unnecessary. Over the years of reading the Bible I came to the conclusion that without this genealogy the total story would be incomplete. To some extent I find the genealogy comforting in that Yeshua was once just like me, from a family of mortal, fallible people. On the other hand, I find the genealogy to be comforting because it serves as a traceable roadmap to salvation, just as was prophesized from history to present.

Let me be real with you now, just you and me here… One on one, worry and anxiety, depression and habitual sorrow is overtaking so many people in this society today. If that describes you, maybe you've suffered a loss that you just cannot find your way through, I believe the following passage from the Book of Matthew might be just for you…

Overcoming Worry with Trust

> [25] "So I say to you, do not worry about your life—what you will eat or drink, or about your body, what you will wear. Isn't life more than food and the body more than clothing?
>
> [26] "**Look at the birds of the air.** They do not sow or reap or gather into barns; **yet your Father in heaven feeds them.** **_Are you not of more value than they?_** [27] And which of you by worrying can add a single hour to his life? [a] [28] And why do you worry about clothing? Consider the lilies of the field, how they grow. They neither toil nor spin. [29] Yet I tell you that not even Solomon in all his glory clothed himself like one of these. [b] [30] Now if in this way God clothes the grass—which is here today and thrown into the furnace tomorrow—will He not much more clothe you, O you of little faith?
>
> [31] "Therefore do not worry, saying, 'What will we eat?' or 'What will we drink?' or 'What will we wear?' [32] For the pagans eagerly pursue all these things; yet your Father in heaven knows that you need all these. [33] But seek first the kingdom of God and His righteousness, and all these things shall be added to you. [34] Therefore do not worry about tomorrow, for tomorrow will worry about itself. Each day has enough trouble of its own."

Tree of Life Version (TLV)
Tree of Life (TLV) Translation of the Bible. Copyright © 2015 by The Messianic Jewish Family Bible Society.

I am a photographer and I am privileged to have my work hanging in homes and offices and spaces all over the world. If you know my work, you will know that I find being in nature tantamount to being in the greatest sanctuary in this realm. The birds of the air, the waves of the sea, the forests and mountains speak of their Creator, and ours. He provides for them just what they need, and so He does also for me. Worry less by trusting Heavenly Father. Seems crazy in this world, but the following is why we can with confidence, trust Him.

It is incredulous that Jesus Christ has to endure so much for me so early in His earthly life. It seems unfair that Jesus would have to suffer ridicule when He was so "good." He did so much good for so many, healing hearts, souls, and bodies. He raised the dead and yet He pulsed ever quicker to the cross to die Himself. It just does not seem right. Why would He look from the cross and think of His love for me, and remain on that wooden cross, hewn from a tree that Jesus' Father created when He did not have to? He chose me and He chose you. Jesus felt you and I were worth all the pain and suffering, the torture and death... so WE would have hope.

In the process Yeshua amazed the Pharisees, taught the disciples, and loosed the bonds of sin from people who had no hope. People just like me. We are taught, warned, and healed by Jesus, the unlikely King from Nazareth. Now, knowing this Truth I am held to a higher standard to not just KNOW, but also more importantly DO.

Matthew 7:15-20 Tree of Life Version (TLV)

Judging the Fruit

> 15 *"Watch out for false prophets,[a] who come to you in sheep's clothing but inwardly are ravenous wolves. 16 You will recognize them by their fruit. Grapes aren't gathered from thorn bushes or figs from thistles, are they? 17 Even so, every good tree **produces** good fruit, but the rotten tree produces bad fruit. 18 A good tree cannot produce bad fruit, nor can a rotten tree produce good fruit. 19 Every tree that **does not produce** good fruit is chopped down and thrown into the fire. 20 So then, you will recognize them by their fruit.*

Tree of Life (TLV) Translation of the Bible. Copyright © 2015 by The Messianic Jewish Family Bible Society.

Knowing is not tantamount to doing. Being a knower is not being a doer.

Yeshua lived, died, and rose again to Life not so I can just know. Jesus Christ subjected Himself to that which He did not have to for us to know the truth, but to DO the gospel.

Let me add this for you to consider. Earlier I spoke of needless worry in our lives… Some of us recreate God in our own image, and in so doing; we limit Him in our minds to that which we experience in the day-to-day lives we live, people disappointing us daily. We conceive of God less each time someone in our lives hurts us because we subconsciously believe that what is here on earth is what is in Heaven.

I want you to remember, much of our unbelief is tied to the failure of fellow mortals and to be honest with you… "To be forgiven, you must be forgiving." We are often stuck in our resentment and lack of forgiveness that we cannot feel the forgiveness and mercy and grace of God. The message is simple, put your hurts habits and hang ups down once and for all. The best place to leave them is at the foot of the Cross.

Matthew 25:14
Parable of the Talents

14"For it is like a man about to go on a journey. He called his own servants and handed over his possessions to them.

*15To one he gave five talents, to another two, and to another one, **each according to his own ability**. Then he went on his journey.*

16"Immediately the one who had received the five talents went and traded with them and gained five more.

17In the same way, the one with two gained two more.

18But the one who received one went off and dug a hole in the ground and hid his master's money.

19"Now after a long time, the master of those servants came and settled accounts with them.

20The one who had received the five talents came up and brought another five talents, saying, 'Master, you handed me five talents. Look, I've gained five more.'

21His master said to him, 'Well done, good and faithful servant! You were faithful with a little, so I'll put you in charge of much. Enter into your master's joy!'

22"The one who had received the two talents also came up and said, 'Master, you handed me two talents. Look, I've gained two more.'

23His master said to him, 'Well done, good and faithful servant! You were faithful with a little, so I'll put you in charge of much. Enter into your master's joy!'

24"Then the one who had received the one talent also came up and said, 'Master, I knew that you are a hard man, reaping where you didn't sow and gathering where you scattered no seed.

25So I was afraid, and I went off and hid your talent in the ground. See, you have what is yours.'

26"But his master responded, 'You wicked, lazy servant! You knew that I reap where I didn't sow and gather where I scattered no seed?

27Then you should have brought my money to the brokers, and when I came I would have received it back with interest.

28Therefore take the talent away from him, and give it to the one who has the ten talents.

29For to the one who has, more shall be given, and he shall have an abundance. But from the one who does not have, even what he does have shall be taken away.

30Throw the worthless servant out, into the outer darkness where there will be weeping and gnashing of teeth.'"

Faithfulness with the gifts is the goal...

Colossians 3:23-25
*²³ Whatever you do, work at it **from the soul**, as for the Lord and not for people. ²⁴ For you know that from the Lord you will receive the inheritance as a reward. It is to the Lord Messiah you are giving service. ²⁵ For the one doing wrong will be paid back for what he did wrong, and there is no favoritism.*

Whatever you do, do it with everything you've got as though you are working for the Lord, not you or the people around you... It is most often most difficult to "work for the Lord" because the feedback is so muted, and we are a very risk and reward life...

Modern paradigm looks for a little work, and IMMEDIATE reward... But with God, it often doesn't happen that way. No one would smoke cigarettes if the by the butt of the dart tumors started popping out of your body... in the same way, but from the positive; we don't find immediate reward from SERVING the Lord.... We most often seek immediate accolade for the littlest thing we do for man....

In the story of the talents we come to realize that 'comparing talents' is a self perpetuating and nearly always devastating pursuit. For purposes of accuracy, one talent was worth 6000 denarii.

Here is an important tidbit that is REALLY critical to full understanding this parable and what it REALLY means… What are 6000 denarii? 6000 denarii is almost 16 YEARS of wages! So they got one talent guy; I mean, the guy who was entrusted with the just the one talent, ended up lamenting ONLY getting one talent… Lamenting being entrusted with SIXTEEN YEARS of wages?

Before you say, "Whoa! That is a lot of wages!" Let me say, his issue was his comparison to the other people who were entrusted with more talents. He had SIXTEEN years worth of wages, more than he could have ever gotten on his own in less than sixteen years and he was complaining because he got less than the others.

The thing is, God won't do for us what we can and should do for ourselves. But, can He trust us? Can He trust us with a little, or a lot? The real truth is, can WE trust ourselves?

Book of the Bible – Mark

Author - Mark
Date of Writing – A.D. 60-70
Number of Chapters - 16
To Whom Written – Romans and Gentiles, to the larger audience, us.
Purpose of the Writing – We are presented with Jesus of Nazareth as God's Suffering Servant who redeemed the world.

My Personal Summary–

The birth of Jesus, the Life of Jesus, the message of Jesus, the death of Jesus, and the resurrection of Jesus of Nazareth; all held within this great Book of Mark.

One of my favorite characters of the Bible is John the Baptist or, in his actual name, Yochanon the Immerser. John the Baptist was uniquely bold in his call for holiness and repentance. John the Baptist's message was one of dynamic obedience. He obeyed his call from God unto his own death. Despite appearing crazy or as modernity would call him, un-pc; John the Baptist boldly and wildly told the story of a coming Messiah, One greater than him.

Though the death of John the Baptist was noted almost as a footnote he did what he was sent to do. John did not speak of the cross Yeshua would bear; however, he knew prophecy and inasmuch as knowledge is often mistaken to bring power, the Baptist knew his fate was set, and so forward he preached.

Jesus was human; He was baptized because His Father commanded it so. Jesus was fully human; He was tempted as a full human and the Divine and yet He did not sin. Jesus was human; yet He ministered and healed the obscure in obscurity because the Father said to do so in His Name. Yeshua attracted controversy nearly everywhere He went because He was original. He was dynamic. He was Divine and yet human. He is God's Son and though Mark takes us on a very succinct journey, he entices us often with his exhortation, "immediately." I am reminded to act immediately upon the leading of God, to obey without delay.

Power to Pardon the Paralyzed

1 When He returned to Capernaum after some days, it was heard that He was at the house.

2 So many were gathered that there was no longer room for them even outside the door. He kept proclaiming the word to them.

3 Some people came bringing to Him a paralyzed man, carried by four men.

4 When they couldn't get near Yeshua because of the crowd, they removed the roof where He was. After digging through, they lowered the mat on which the paralyzed man was lying.

*5 Yeshua, seeing **their faith**, said to the paralyzed man, "Son, your sins are forgiven."*

6 But some of the Torah scholars were sitting there, questioning in their hearts,

7 "Why does this fellow speak like this? He blasphemes! Who can pardon sins but God alone?"

8 Immediately Yeshua, knowing in His spirit that they were raising questions this way within themselves, said to them, "Why are you questioning these things in your hearts?

9 Which is easier, to say to the paralyzed man, 'Your sins are forgiven,' or to say, 'Get up, and take your mat and walk'?

10 But so you may know that the Son of Man has authority to pardon sins on earth...." He tells the paralyzed man,

*11 "I tell you, **get up**, take your mat and go home!"*

*12 At once the man got up, took his mat, and walked before them all. They were all astonished and glorified God, saying, **"We've never seen anything like this!"***

We've never seen anything like this, this Jesus. The world never saw anything like Yeshua Hamashiach... and never will again, until.... Until the day He returns.

Action, Jesus Christ has a bias toward action, as did these men who were the truest of friends to the paralytic. These men had a bias toward action, I mean; they ripped a roof off of a house for Pete's sake; well, I don't know if the paralyzed guy's name was Pete, but you get the point! Isn't that really how faith works? Faith has a bias toward faith, real *"roof ripping"* faith. How long has it been since you would rip a roof off, in faith.

The Book of Mark teaches the importance of placing your faith in Christ immediately and fully. Jesus Christ is trustworthy with our faith because He trod the rocky path with grace and mercy, and truth to the death.

Book of the Bible – Luke
Author –Likely Luke
Date of Writing – A.D. 59-63
Number of Chapters - 24
To Whom Written – Theophilus, Romans and Gentiles, to the larger audience, us.
Purpose of the Writing – To strengthen the faith of believers and to commend the preaching of gospel of Jesus Christ to the entire world.

My Personal Summary–

This is a most clear telling of the way of salvation through none other than Yeshua. Luke was especially Jewish in his reporting of events surrounding the Christ. Luke was so Jewish, yet he was also very inviting toward Gentiles. Luke tells us through his account of Jesus' life that family was important to Jesus and that Yeshua wanted us to know family is important to us too.

We are also clearly advised in the Book of Luke that prayer **with** the Father is incredibly important. Women, we are shown are important to Christ, even in a time when women were severely marginalized by society. Equally marginalized were the poor, and Jesus we are told, loves the poor and ministers gently to them. Through this book we are told Jesus cared for sinners, which relieves me, a sinner.

Luke writes masterfully the story of Zacharias and Elizabeth miraculous conception and birth of John the Baptist, cousin of Yeshua and the Immaculate Conception and birth of Yeshua, the Christ. Two stories inextricably tied to one another, for our good.

In the time before Yeshua was revealed in a baby there were great struggles as there are today. However; we see that God gifts us with the Christ, the Messiah, and the Long Awaited One. In Him we have hope. Luke beautifully describes the temptation of Jesus but it is in v4: 13 that he gives us the completion of the temptation which hinges on one word for me, *"every."* Yeshua was exposed to every temptation, and yet we are given a Savior that did not fall, He did not fail and in this The Messiah we can rest assured.

This highlights what is first said in v1: 2 "… eyewitnesses and servants of the Logos… or the Word." Elizabeth and Mary obeyed, their husbands obeyed and were "servants of the Logos" and thus we have an opportunity to be saved. Soli Deo Gloria!

Consider this as we look back at The Book of Luke Chapter 5… *"Immediately."*

Luke 5 Tree of Life Version (TLV)

Calling Fishermen at the *Kinneret*

> *5 It happened that the crowds were pressing upon Yeshua to* hear the word of God as He was standing by the Lake of *Kinneret,* *2 when He saw two boats standing beside the lake. Now the fishermen had left them and were washing the nets.* *3 Getting into one of the boats, Simon's boat, Yeshua* asked him to push out a ways from the land. Then sitting down, He taught the crowds from the boat.
>
> *4 When He had finished speaking, He said to Simon, "Go out into the deep water, and let down your nets for a catch."*
>
> *5 Simon replied, "Master, we've worked hard all night and caught nothing. But at Your word I will let down the nets." 6 When they had done this, they caught so many fish that their nets began to break. 7 So they signaled to their partners in the other boat to come and help them. They came*

and filled both boats so full that they began to sink. *⁸ But when Simon Peter saw this, he fell down at Yeshua's knees, saying, "Go away from me, Master, for I am a sinful man!"* ⁹ *For amazement had gripped him and all who were with him, over the catch of fish they had netted;* ¹⁰ *so also Jacob and John, Zebedee's sons, who were partners with Simon.*

But Yeshua said to Simon, "Do not be afraid. From now on, you will be catching men." ¹¹ *So when they had brought the boats to the landing, they left everything and followed Him.*

Yeshua Heals and News Spreads

¹² *Now while Yeshua was in one of the towns, a man covered with tzara'at appeared. And when he saw Yeshua, he fell on his face and begged Him, saying, "Master, if You are willing, You can make me clean."*

¹³ *Yeshua stretched out His hand and touched him, saying, "I am willing. Be cleansed!" Immediately, the tzara'at left him.* ¹⁴ *Yeshua ordered him to tell no one, but commanded him, "Go and show yourself to the kohen.* [a] *Then bring an offering for your cleansing, just as Moses commanded, as a testimony to them."*

¹⁵ *But the news about Yeshua was spreading all the more, and many crowds were coming together to hear and to be healed of their diseases.* ¹⁶ *Yet He would often slip away into the wilderness and pray.*

Crowds Gather from the Galilee, Judea, and Jerusalem

¹⁷ *Now on one of those days, Yeshua* was teaching. Pharisees and *Torah* scholars were sitting there, who had come from every village of the Galilee and Judea, as well as from Jerusalem. And *Adonai's* power to heal was

in Him. *18 And behold, men were carrying a paralyzed man on a stretcher, trying to bring him in and place him before Yeshua. 19 But **when they found no way** to bring him in because of the crowd, **they went up on the roof** and let him down with his stretcher through the tiles, right in the middle before Yeshua. 20 When He saw their faith, He said, "Man, your sins **are** forgiven."*

21 Then the Torah scholars and the Pharisees began to question, saying, "Who is this fellow speaking blasphemies? Who can pardon sins but God alone?"

*22 Yeshua, **knowing** their thoughts, replied to them, "Why are you raising questions in your hearts? 23 Which is easier, to say, '**Your sins are forgiven** you,' or to say, '**Get up and walk**'? 24 But so you may know that the Son of Man **has authority** on earth to pardon sins. . . ." He said to the paralyzed one, "I tell you, get up and take your cot, and go home!"*

*25 **Immediately** he got up before them, picked up what he had been lying on, and went home, glorifying God. 26 Astonishment took hold of them, and they glorified God and all were filled with awe, saying, "We've seen incredible things today!"*

This speaks of the undeniable power of NOW and the compelling power of immediately.

We see this bias toward action now later I Scripture, in several coinciding locations.... Just as Luke Chapter 5 speaks of *"Immediately,"* Peter took charge to choose another who should replace Judas Iscariot after his paid betrayal demonstrating that no matter what, the work of Christ forges on. We must not become complacent or tired in service to Yeshua. There is power in the immediate. There is power in doing it NOW, believing NOW, and acting on your faith, NOW!

Book of the Bible - The Gospel According to the Apostle John

Author –John, the disciple whom Jesus loved (13:23)

Date of Writing – Between 50 and 70 A.D.

Number of Chapters - 21

To Whom Written – Gentile Christians needing a boost in their faith and to those without a saving knowledge of Yeshua.

Purpose of the Writing – Jn 20:30*Therefore many other signs Jesus also performed in the presence of the disciples, which are not written in this book; 31 but these have been written so that you may believe that Jesus is the Christ, the Son of God; and that believing you may have life in His name.*

My Personal Summary–

Whenever I read the Gospel According to John I actually cry. This book, more than any other profoundly impacts me to tears because it is inscribed on my very soul. I am so deeply moved because the words of John, the apostle who saw Christ, who loved and was loved by Yeshua writes with such deep love for his Savior that I am convicted by my lack of depth of faith that I must weep, and after weeping I am renewed and inspired to love God more deeply, more effectively.

John loved and loves his Jesus when he writes the words of this book, and when he revisits the torture, death and resurrection of his Savior he cries, much like me. I never physically saw Yeshua, but I see Him through the words of John.

This book was written that *"we may believe that Jesus is the Christ, the Son of God, and that by believing we may have life in His name."* [Emphasis mine]

Vibrant LIFE! Not constant sorrow, wringing of hands, worry and fear. Life is now and here worshipping God the Father, serving Christ.

It all started with the Word, which in Greek is, logos. The logos of God was the beginning and is the beginning. Everything that is good comes from the wellspring of Life of God. We are given what we need for here on Earth from this abundant wellspring and John shows us what we are given is more than what we ever need.

The Word of God in the form of a Man lived among us for thirty-three years and in that short blip in time changed all of time. In obedience to prophecy, John the Baptist claimed Christ before even one miracle was recorded. John testified boldly that THE One who is come is greater than he is, and he was clear that we are to follow Him and Him alone.

> **John 1:14-18 Tree of Life Version (TLV)**
> *14 And the **Word**(God, separate and distinct)became flesh (Jesus)and tabernacle among us. We looked upon His glory,[a] the glory of the one and only[b] from the Father, full of grace and truth.*
>
> *15 John testifies about Him. He cried out, saying, "This is He of whom I said, 'The One* (Jesus Christ) *who comes after me is above me, because He existed before me.'"* (John the Baptist was older in earthly natural years, but Jesus Christ was of The Father) *16 Out of His fullness, we have all received grace on top of grace. 17 Torah* was given through Moses; grace and truth came through *Yeshua* the Messiah. *18 No one has ever seen God; but the one and only God,[c]* in the Father's embrace, has made Him known.

Jesus is God and though I am over my word goal, I must say this:

Thank God for the many parables, which instruct and inspire.
Thank God for the suffering and sorrow of Jesus Christ.
Thank God for His mercy and grace this is more than sufficient for me.

Within this Book of John we hear of the performance of the first recorded miracle of Jesus at the wedding feast of Cana started a ticking clock that would not end until Yeshua was tortured and murdered, and resurrected from the sin grave I helped dig for Him! Soli Deo Gloria!

The many healings by Yeshua are described, the preaching and parables of Jesus are recounted, and yet, there were so many more exploits that John tells us it wouldn't all fit in the world's books. I cannot wait to ask John and even Yeshua Himself about all those others!

Book of the Bible – Acts of the Apostles
Author –Luke the physician
Date of Writing – A.D. 63-70
Number of Chapters - 28
To Whom Written – Theophilus, the same as in the Gospel of Luke.
Purpose of the Writing – This critically important book presents an historical account of Christian origins, the founding of the church, spread of the gospel and the inner workings of the church, as it should be.

My Personal Summary–

Luke knew there would be problems and persecutions of the Christians within the church of Yeshua, the One you're most familiar being called Jesus. Many of the disciples and apostles and followers of Christ died simply because they would not deny the resurrection of Christ. They could have lied, and all they had to stipulate to is that yes, He was a healer, preacher, teacher, but NOT One Who rose after death! The Disciples refused to live in a lie, so they died horrific deaths for the Truth.

Luke knew this suffering was only the beginning of persecutions for Christ and he wanted us to have instructions on how to get through them and to properly serve Jesus and His people.

Luke understood that Yeshua' s commission was to include those outside of the lands of the Hebrew people and the Aramaic language and thus, he spoke in the language of the people to whom he was speaking. He was a master at reaching his audience right at their level. WE must become better at speaking the proper language to which we are speaking if we have any hope of understanding. You wouldn't take a Mandarin interpreter to deliver a speech to a German speaking audience. Why? Because they simply wouldn't understand and would quickly stop listening. They would tune me out.

While the Old Testament has a strong theocratic (God ruling) purpose teaching the people that God will rule the world and that Jesus would reign over His nation of Israel, the soteriological (or doctrinal) purpose of the New Testament is to tell us that God saves peoples and societies through Jesus Christ and that those of the church would be saved through Him.

In Jesus **all** of God's purposes are fulfilled.

How crushing it must have been to "lose" Jesus just as the disciples were starting to understand what He was saying? So too, how amazing it must have been for those in attendance at the ascension to see Jesus ascend and to know they must carry the cross from now forward, until Jesus returns. They really had no idea when Jesus was coming back; however, Jesus told them not to check their watches and to scour the sky for signs, and He would come when He comes, when the time, His time was perfect and chosen.

Book of the Bible - Romans
Author - the Apostle Paul
Date of Writing – A.D. 57
Number of Chapters – 16
To Whom Written – The church at Rome
Purpose of the Writing – To prepare the way for his visit to Rome and Spain, present a system of salvation to a church without having experienced apostolic teaching, and to explain the relationship between Jews and Gentile's in God's plan of redemption and to release the Jewish Christ-followers from dietary laws and sacred days.[5]

---

[5] NASB Study Bible Romans Introduction was of great help in this aspect of the project.

My Personal Summary–

The Epistle of Paul to the Romans was called by Coleridge to be the *"most profound work in existence."* No other apostle convicts me for my lukewarm faith more than does the apostle Paul. Zodhiates succinctly states, *"God does not only declare us justified, but makes us just."*

> Romans 5:19 *For just as through the disobedience of one man, many were made sinners, so also through the obedience of one man, many will be set right forever.*[d]

We are often heard conceding to sin as though we are powerless against sin, yet the Word tells us that sin, hurts habits and hang-ups do not own us. Yet while we feel powerless, we are not without access to the ultimate power against sin, to overcome our hurts habits and hang-ups. In our weakness we are strong so long as we stand in the strength of God, through the Holy Spirit as given to us when Yeshua trod to the cross in His own bloody footprints traceable only to our sins.

As I am a Gentile,the very Jewish observant Paul gives me hope in emphasizing that Abraham was justified by faith and not by works alone. If the patriarch of the Jews was justified by faith even before circumcision, salvation can also be mine! Jesus Christ was delivered of His own volition to the cross in my place, for my sins, and He was raised for my salvation. My only hope is in Christ and in that I may be happy and be influenced by the Holy Spirit to exude pure joy in my salvation.

Modern society, particularly the post-modern emergent church speaks often of the acquisition of wealth and well being in terms of "favor, lack, and abundance." These are the buzzwords of the new era. However, Paul speaks of the mercy and judgment of God as being proper and without question.

Our salvation starts and ends with God's grace and our call, as believers we are to pursue a holy life, though the word "holiness" is co-opted by liberals as "judgmental and mean-spirited."

Paul demonstrates clearly that God is the Perfect judge, and He will judge us according to our soul condition and the fruits of our faith, the work we do as evidence of our conversion. Before our conversion we were slaves to our sin, (6:19) and now we must surrender ourselves to uprightness, no matter how difficult of unpopular that may be these days, eternal life awaits the sanctified (6:22).

Book of the Bible – The First Epistle of Paul to the Corinthians
Author –The Apostle Paul
Date of Writing – A.D 96
Number of Chapters - 16
To Whom Written – The Corinthian church
Purpose of the Writing – The Church at Corinth wrote a letter to Paul asking for guidance and instruction on several major struggles they were having in their church. Those problems included church discipline and practice. "How to 'do' church."

My Personal Summary–

Paul established the church at Corinth during his second missionary journey and it is clear, this church was dear to the Apostle Paul. As a labor of love, Paul stayed in Corinth for eighteen months and upon his leaving, there arose many problems of gross immorality, lawsuits between Christians, and a myriad of problems relating to the living of a Christian life. Paul was just the man for the job. They were off the chain and for the most part, they didn't actually KNOW how to DO church.

These people lived as pagans before their conversions and as such, there was much to address the pains of adjustment from the dark past into the light of living in Christ.

The primary lessons for me in reading this great book are; God's is wiser than all human thought, Jesus' resurrection is central to my faith in Christ and without the resurrection as truth, the rest of my effort is wasted, and finally, sometimes discipline must be meted out in the church. This letter from Paul dealt wisely on how to live, and how to "be the church."

In the outset of the letter Paul affirms the preaching of the cross as the power of God through the cross. The crucifixion and resurrection are the central differences in faith in God and pagan faith. Paul dealt directly with the issues of Christian marriage and his direction on divorce more deftly than most modern counselors, yet he did so succinctly.

There were many doctrinal disputes, which were obscuring the mission of the church, and in a trendy town like Corinth it is reasonable to compare Corinth to our cultural centers today. As such, the hip, trendy and cool folks who want more to be no different with society than to proclaim the cross were called out then, and today. While we master the languages of our listeners, we must be sure we do not change the Message.

The Holy Spirit is as available to me today as it was to the people of Corinth and the Holy Spirit moved Paul to begin his correspondence with the Corinthians with encouragement and commendation for what they were doing well. Pastors today would do well to remember Paul's example. We must lead from the positive without fearing to deal with the harsh negatives that arise in the modern assembly of jacked up pastors and people. I am as jacked up a pastor as you will ever likely find, but I know this, we had better be REAL with one another or we are just playing church.

It is utterly foundational to living Christ-like is to do what we are supposed to do, what we are instructed to do, or our labor will be in vain and we will be rewarded accordingly.

No One Is Acceptable

> *1 Then what is the advantage of being Jewish? Or what is the benefit of circumcision?*

2 Much in every way. First of all, they were entrusted with the sayings of God.

3 So what if some did not trust? Will their lack of faith nullify God's faithfulness?

4 May it never be! Let God be true even if every man is a liar, as it is written, "that You may be righteous in Your words and prevail when You are judged."

5 But if our unrighteousness demonstrates the righteousness of God, what shall we say? God is not unrighteous to inflict wrath, is He? (I am speaking in human terms.)

6 May it never be! For otherwise, how will God judge the world?

7 But if by my lie the truth of God abounds to His glory, why am I still judged as a sinner?

8 And why not say, "Let us do evil, so that good may come" —just as we are being slandered and as some claim that we say. Their condemnation is deserved!

9 What then? Are we better than they? No, not at all. For we have already made the case that all—both Jewish and Greek people—are under sin.

10 As it is written, "There is no one righteous—no, not one.

11 There is no one who understands, no one who seeks after God.

12 All have turned aside; together they have become worthless. There is no one who does good—no, not even one!

13 Their throat is an open grave; with their tongues they keep deceiving. The poison of vipers is under their lips.

14 Their mouth is full of cursing and bitterness.

15 Their feet are swift to shed blood.

16 Ruin and misery are in their paths,

17 and the way of shalom they have not known.

18 There is no fear of God before their eyes."

19 Now we know that whatever the Torah says, it says to those within the *Torah, so that every mouth may be shut and the whole world may become accountable to God.*

20 For no human, on the basis of Torah observance, will be set right in His sight—for through the *Torah* comes awareness of sin.

How God Accepts Us

21 But now God's righteousness apart from the Torah has been revealed, to which the *Torah* and the Prophets bear witness—

22 namely, the righteousness of God through putting trust in Messiah Yeshua, to all who keep on trusting. For there is no distinction,

23 for all have sinned and fall short of the glory of God.

24 They are set right as a gift of His grace, through the redemption that is in Messiah Yeshua.

25 God set forth Yeshua as an atonement, through faith in His blood, to show His righteousness in passing over sins already committed.

26 Through God's forbearance, He demonstrates His righteousness at the present time—that He Himself is just and also the justifier of the one who puts his trust in Yeshua.

27 Where, then, is boasting? It is excluded. By what principle? Of works? No, but by the principle of faith.

28 For we consider a person to be set right apart from Torah observance.

29 Is God the God of the Jewish people only? Is He not also the God of the Gentiles? Yes, of the Gentiles also.

30 Since God is One, He will set right the circumcised by faith and the uncircumcised through faith.

31 Do we then nullify the Torah through faithfulness? May it never be! On the contrary, we uphold the Torah.

Book of the Bible – The Second Epistle of Paul to the Corinthians
Author – The Apostle Paul
Date of Writing – A.D. 55
Number of Chapters – 13
To Whom Written – The church in Corinth and the Christians throughout Achaia – Roman province in Greece.
Purpose of the Writing – To combat the infiltration of false teachers who sought to usurp Paul's authority and validity as an Apostle of Christ. Paul urged the church at Corinth to deal with the troublemakers within the church. Paul minces no words.

My Personal Summary–

The Apostle Paul is a formidable leader within the early church with ripples evident even today. Paul's greeting is customarily cordial with an invocation of peace that can come only from God the Father and the Lord Jesus Christ. After the cordiality comes the righteous fire so characteristic of the Apostle Paul.

Paul also gives praise directly to God for sustaining and comforting him in his affliction. Paul is adept at teaching shared suffering and comfort alike to a church that was falling prey to great struggles and minor discomforts alike. The great apostle restates his basis for integrity and forgives his offender in the church. Many folks portray Paul as a stern and uncaring man yet the facts do not bear that claim out.

The Apostle Paul recounts many of the events that transpired in his ministry and missionary journey without whining or complaining, but all the while giving Christ the glory.

Paul was keenly aware of his detractors; however, he focused on the point which is stated most clearly in **2 Corinthians 5:9-10:**

> *2Co 5:9 Therefore we also have as our ambition, whether at home or absent, to be pleasing to Him.*
>
> *10 For we must all appear before the judgment seat of Christ, so that each one may be recompensed for his deeds in the body, according to what he has done, whether good or bad.*

Whether alive or dead when Jesus returns we must seek to please God and we will be measured by the deeds we have done, good or bad.

Book of the Bible – The Epistle of Paul to the Galatians
Author – The Apostle Paul
Date of Writing – The North Galatian theory states A.D. 53-57. The South Galatian theory states A.D. 51-53.
Number of Chapters – 6
To Whom Written – According to whichever theory you ascribe, the church of Northern Galatia, or Southern Galatia.
Purpose of the Writing – Legalism and rituals endemic to the Jews were not being observed by the Gentile converts to Christ, much to the Pharisees dismay. Paul addresses this and other issues which were antithetical to the primary mission, to preach the cross and resurrection of Yeshua. Further, to establish that it is by faith alone that we are to live within the freedom of the Spirit.

My Personal Summary–

The lynchpin of Martin Luther's writings and theology is held in Paul's letter to the Galatians; man is justified only by grace through faith in the risen Christ and not through any works of our own. Our obedience to the precepts of the Holy Scriptures is the demonstration of our true faith and conversion. We are empowered to full obedience through faith in the propitiation or atonement of Christ on the cross for us and that we live only through the strength and power of Yeshua and the Holy Spirit within us.

No matter how obedient we may try to be, nothing short of the grace and mercy of Jesus Christ will declare us righteous and the relentless pursuit of perfection (which I am guilty of) in the name of honoring Christ with our lives. As proof, I cite this work you now hold in your hands, which I have completed nearly two times and have not, submitted it because I felt it unworthy of a perfect Savior.

Paul spoke contextually to the Galatians; however, his message is pertinent to the modern church. We err on both sides of the law; either we want nothing but post-modern emergent theology which is weak and baseless, or we pursue legalism dressed as tradition. The modern church seems to struggle to find the sweet spot of faith and practice.

Paul spoke to the freedom we could have if only we lived by faith. Christ died so that we may be set free and not so that we can make up endless man-made laws to measure our obedience.

Freedom Based on Favor

1For freedom, Messiah set us free—so stand firm, and do not be burdened by a yoke of slavery again.

2Listen—I, Paul, tell you that if you let yourselves be circumcised, Messiah will be of no benefit to you.

3Again I testify to every man who lets himself be circumcised, that he is obligated to keep the whole Torah.

4You who are trying to be justified by Torah have been cut off from Messiah; you have fallen away from grace.

5For through the Ruach, by faith, we eagerly wait for the hope of righteousness.

6For in Messiah Yeshua, neither circumcision nor uncircumcision has any meaning—but only trust and faithfulness expressing itself through love.

Paul teaches also the act of restoration of the fallen, which we in the modern circles of faith too often forget to observe.

Book of the Bible – The Epistle of Paul to the Ephesians

Author – The Apostle Paul

Date of Writing – A.D. 60

Number of Chapters – 6

To Whom Written – A circular letter with emphasis on the church at Ephesus

Purpose of the Writing – To expand the horizons and thinking of his readers so they would grasp God's eternal purpose for the church and to establish the high benchmark God has for us.

My Personal Summary–

Through God's grace to us we are reconciled to Him through Christ and inasmuch as we are all recipients of God's infinite grace and mercy, we are also one body, together reaping the reward of that grace. In our daily lives, boring or exciting as they may be, we are to live for Christ and in Christ alone. In other words, we MUST depend on and trust Christ fully for all aspects of our lives... If you want to feel Him close to you, you must get closer and closer to Him each day.

We as the church must find the words of the apostle comforting and yet challenging at the same time. Through our gifts given to us from God we are empowered to minister to one another, when we are strong or even more importantly, when we are weak. We are to be united as one church all pursuing holiness in all that we do and say. We are to help one another, not tear one another down. We are to lift one another, encourage one another and hold each other accountable.

We are given the great gift of prayer as a means of communicating **with** God through the Holy Spirit in as Christ is the Head of the church there must be a drive toward purity and holiness, though we shall never attain either before we kneel before Yeshua Himself. I get it; that is super difficult and frankly, most times it seems a feckless pursuit for me... But the drive toward knowing Him better demands it so that we can know Him better, to understand. It isn't a contest, or a comparison thing. That is where we get into so much trouble... We can never measure up on our own.

Paul tells the church then and now that we are redeemed and that the redeemed of the Lord should say so. Our lives, not our mouths must give the greatest testimony congruent with God's grace given to us. Sin was and is our death, and only in Christ are we made alive. Paul speaks firmly on his authority as a 'prisoner of Christ Jesus' for the sake of the Gentiles (3:1). His authority is not gained in legalistic observance because he writes he is the 'least of all saints' (3:8). So am I.

Book of the Bible – The Epistle of Paul to the Philippians
Author – The Apostle Paul
Date of Writing – A.D. 61
Number of Chapters – 4
To Whom Written – The church at Philippi
Purpose of the Writing – This letter was written to thank and encourage the church at Philippi for their support during his detention in Rome, to lift them up as they will soon face persecution in the Name of Jesus Christ and to commend Timothy and Epaphroditus to the church at Philippi. Finally, this letter was written to warn of legalists and libertines among them.

My Personal Summary–

Jesus put on the dirty clothes of human skin and as a man He made us pure through His death on the cross for our sake. Jesus died as a cursed man, on a gruesome cross meant for the worst of mankind, me, yet He was the best of all Men.

Paul tells us to look outside of ourselves so that we may know the suffering and sorrow, and even joy of our fellow members. Paul tells us directly to be like Christ, have the attitude of Christ, the heart of Christ. We should be humble like Christ and not grumble in our daily life of service unto God. We should seek purity as Jesus was pure in the flesh in spite of the perverse generation during which He walked the earth.

I believe Paul knew we would tire of craning our necks Heaven-ward beckoning Christ's return in the light of morning without changing residence as the sun sets on another day. Our work for Christ will not be in vain and at some point of God's perfect choosing, Yeshua will return to set it right. In the meantime, I am to live right depending on God to do a good work in me.

Timothy and Epaphroditus were of the same mind as Paul and in commending them publicly; he gave us a great example to follow. We must be dependable, strong, sanctified and persistent and no matter the sorrow or struggle, we must be filled with joy that we share with others.

Book of the Bible – The Epistle of Paul to the Colossians
Author – The Apostle Paul
Date of Writing – A.D. 60
Number of Chapters – 4
To Whom Written – The church at Colossae
Purpose of the Writing – The letter was written to refute the Colossian heresy, exalting Christ as the very image of God and the Head of the church.

My Personal Summary–

Our human mind was made by God, which we think with while standing on the ground that God created, breathing air God created, living life only by His grace and yet we continue to rely upon our human philosophy instead of Jesus Christ the Messiah.

The heresies of the time included Gnosticism, which separated matter from thought. They further thought matter was evil and the matter they denied was the life, ministry, death and resurrection of Jesus Christ. They identified themselves in contrasting philosophies; to deny all personal pleasure and joy, and the other to hedonistically indulge in all perceived to be pleasure. This is not much different than modern society, or the church.

False teaching was present in Colossae as it is in the United States and as Paul warns the Colossians, we must warn Americans of false teachers. False teaching may come from something as simple as what we should, or should not eat or what day we should Sabbath. We are in the world, but we needn't be of the world and as such, we in our 'new selves' we must set our minds on the things of Christ, not those of this earth.

Our mouths are to mirror our hearts in being pure because the peace of Christ dwells within us. We need to be about praising God in song, prayer and not about bickering about what color the pew cushions should be. If we are not called to be the preacher, then we must pray for the preachers.

Book of the Bible – The First Epistle of Paul to the Thessalonians
Author – The Apostle Paul
Date of Writing – A.D. 51
Number of Chapters – 4
To Whom Written – The church at Thessalonica
Purpose of the Writing – Because of Paul's immediate departure left many former pagans without Christian support in a society very antagonistic toward followers of the way of Christ. This letter was written to encourage and instruct the new converts in their faith.

My Personal Summary–

A city of over 200,000 mostly Gentiles populated the fledgling church with former pagans who needed direction in their faith that would surely expose them to persecution in the Name of Christ. What of their daily lives when they weren't in the throes of persecution? How were they to live? What type of worker should they be?

Paul prays for the churches in all of the epistles he wrote, how long must his prayer-time have been? In Paul's amazing personal example of dedication to Christ we are given a great example to emulate. The people of Thessalonica turned from pagan, idol worshipping days to serve the one true God and in our media-crazed era, we have many idols to turn from and yet the same true God to turn to.

Paul preaches to the unsaved and saved alike because he loves them, as Christ loves the church and we are to instruct in love, as Yeshua instructs in love. Paul does not speak of 'increase' and 'abundance' in terms of pecuniary gain; rather, he speaks in terms of increasing our love for one another and for Christ. Post-modern emergent churches and prosperity-preachers would do well to reread the writings of the Apostle Paul.

Sanctification and sexual purity are of God and as such, we are, in our salvation through the cross able to rest in the assurance that whether we are alive or dead at the return of Christ, we will be taken up to be with Him forever. While we are here on earth we are to rejoice in everything, be open to the Holy Spirit and abstain from evil. In the will of God our purposes are made known.

Book of the Bible – The Second Epistle of Paul to the Thessalonians
Author – The Apostle Paul
Date of Writing – A.D. 51 or 52
Number of Chapters – 3
To Whom Written – The church at Thessalonica
Purpose of the Writing – To encourage persecuted Christians to remain strong and industrious. Also, some of the beliefs about Yeshua's return were in need of correction.

My Personal Summary–

The Apostle was surely a great leader of men in that he was encouraging, pinpoint accurate in his teaching, and boldly honest in his reproofs. Paul speaks of increasing love for one another, which is what we are reminded to do. In such love we are to encourage one another, as Paul encouraged the church. We are to reproof and hold accountable one another, as Paul did for the church.

This is especially true when we encounter opposition and persecution. In the current presidential administration I fear we will experience persecution, as we have not in years past. Part of the problem of the modern church is that no one is dying for his or her faith in Christ in the United States and we became soft and weak in our faith. We look for comfort rather than sanctification and holiness. Paul knew that times were tough on the early church, and that times will get tough on future Christians. This suffering points to the authenticity of their Kingdom-focus.

Paul tells us to not focus on revenge for those that transgress us, rather to focus on the cross and the honor we are given to suffer for Christ. We are not to be focused on our trials or false teaching; rather we are to honor God. God can speak only a breath (2:8) and the enemies will be slain, first of which is Satan the champion deceiver. We are to stand firm and follow the Truth of the gospel while staying away from unruly people. We must also be disciplined hard-workers who do not gossip or worry about being good when others do wrong.

Book of the Bible – The First Epistle of Paul to Timothy
Author – the Apostle Paul
Date of Writing – A.D. 70 or slightly later
Number of Chapters – 6
To Whom Written – Timothy and the church at Ephesus
Purpose of the Writing – The purpose is to teach on proper church care and to refute false teaching within the church. Part of church care is in the proper selection of the church leaders, which is clearly detailed in this book.

My Personal Summary–

Be aware of the false teachers God's people! Followers of Jesus, beware of false teachers! As though Paul were here among us today, we can nearly hear Paul warning us of false teachers and heretics trying to line their pockets with controversial and wild doctrines surrounding "prosperity," "abundance" and "jubilee." The Apostle Paul warns us to be aware; however he teaches us the basics of selecting good leaders who will not lead us astray while caring for the needs of the church.

The Pastor cannot attend to every need of every person in the church all of the time. Deacons and Trustees can be a pivotal part of the "Jesus Culture" of a church. It is interesting how hip, trendy, and cool churches are so focused on creating a "culture" in the church, but pay lip-service to the culture of Jesus outside of the trendy church walls. The Bible is the guide we must follow to know what our leaders should be, and what our leaders should do, in accordance with God's Word.

As ministers we are bound to a higher standard, which is to include being bold and strong without being disrespectful of each other and the Word. We are to preach the sound gospel, not some flaky whimsical emotionally whipped-up doctrine designed to stroke our egos because of the number of tears in the audience. We are to teach the precepts and fight the good fight of faith while pursuing righteousness and godliness. We must preach the Word!

Book of the Bible – The Second Epistle of Paul to Timothy
Author – The Apostle Paul
Date of Writing – A.D. 63
Number of Chapters – 4
To Whom Written – Timothy, his mentee.
Purpose of the Writing – Paul was lonely and longed for encouragement and brotherhood. Even in his fatigue he was encouraging to other Christians because he knows the hardships that will come with following the teachings of Christ.

My Personal Summary–

The "race" is what we run as members of the Church and this race is an endurance race rather than a sprint. This is also a challenging race with many obstacles because of the persecution a strong Christian is sure to face while standing for Christ.

There was much wrangling over mere words in the church and Paul strongly advises against quibbling over words while a great work needs to be done. Worldly and empty chatter simply leads to ungodliness and provided we study the Word daily, and do what is prescribed; we need not be ashamed to be workers for Christ provided we preach the Word as we were taught.

The Apostle Paul was lonely and I glean concerned regarding securing enough help for his mission work. He needed help and he knew who would be helpful and who would be harmful to his mission. Paul was clear that some folks actually sought to harm him and his mission, yet he is clear to allow God to exact revenge rather than to burn in vengeance himself. The Apostle Paul trusted God and God alone. We too are to trust God alone for all we need. Our home is in Heaven with God the Father and Jesus His Son. Until we reside physically with Christ, we are to preach the Word in its fullness at all times. If we are bickering endlessly when we have an opportunity to witness, we sin against a Holy and just God.

Book of the Bible – The Epistle of Paul the Apostle to Titus
Author – The Apostle Paul
Date of Writing – Between A.D. 63 and 65
Number of Chapters – 3
To Whom Written – Titus
Purpose of the Writing – To authorize and guide Titus in dealing with growing opposition.

My Personal Summary–

The Apostle Paul was nothing if not courteous. Again in this passage Paul greets his audience with kindness and the identification of the God he serves. The Apostle Paul is also consummately loyal to those in whom he sees the true heart for Christ, in this case, Titus.

God knew that the early church would need direction on basic as well as complex matters and as such, He provided a servant, Paul, a venue to instruct the early church on qualified elders, what they are to do in the performance of their office, the signs of a sound church, and what to do when dissention comes into the church.

This book is timely over the ages because for some reason, we squabble over church colors, names, pews padded or not, what hymnal to use, and whether the preacher should speak over twenty minutes or not. The modern church has largely discarded these sage instructions instead choosing to stand only for what the people would like, what would draw the most people, and what revenue streams might appeal to the most people. The church was in some trouble in Paul's time, and it is in much trouble today.

At the heart of a good church is sound doctrine, proper behavior in leadership and congregation and obedience of the Word. The Word cannot be obeyed unless the leaders of the church first follow the directions given in the Epistle of Paul the Apostle to Titus.

Book of the Bible – The Epistle of Paul the Apostle to Philemon

Author – The Apostle Paul
Date of Writing – A.D. 60
Number of Chapters – 1
To Whom Written – Philemon from the church at Colossae.
Purpose of the Writing – To encourage Philemon to forgive and restore Onesimus as though he were Paul himself.

My Personal Summary–

Onesimus was Philemon's runaway slave and in his bid for freedom he found Christ through the ministry of Paul. This devout convert to Christ would have been a great help to the Apostle Paul; however, Paul ever the diplomat was concerned for the relationship of the once slave to the once slave-owner, Philemon.

Though there is nothing about slavery that appeals to me, this beautiful letter of request to the slave-owner speaks greater volumes to me of the character and content of the Apostle Paul and further, the true grace of our redemption from sin through Christ.

While Paul was himself a prisoner of the Romans, he was concerned for Philemon and Onesimus for their uniquely disparate and yet similar positions in life. Philemon was once slave to sin and was now free; or as much as Philemon would permit. Yet Onesimus was a fellow prisoner of Christ and fellow servant of Christ with the Apostle Paul, freed in Christ from what was true physical bondage at the hand of Philemon. These two men, once slave and slave owner were now brothers in Christ redeemed both through the blood and resurrection of Jesus each the same with no distinction for societal placement or dishonor.

Christ redeemed Onesimus and as such, Onesimus was a great help the Apostle Paul, yet Paul felt the need to carefully address the potential resentment Philemon may feel toward Onesimus, his once slave. Paul addressed the church because if Onesimus suddenly returned, what would they say about Philemon or Onesimus? Gossip killed churches then, and it still does today.

Book of the Bible – The Epistle to the Hebrews
Author – Unclear; however, it is apparent that Paul had great influence over this author, if not Paul himself. I do not believe it was Paul.
Date of Writing – Around A.D. 70
Number of Chapters – 14
To Whom Written – The Hebrew Christians who spoke the Greek language.
Purpose of the Writing – To demonstrate a clear doctrine of Christ-centered faith in contrast to the faith of the Old Testament

My Personal Summary–

How then shall we act if not led by God's precepts and Jesus' example and theologically sound instruction? The Hebrew Christians were in constant danger of relapsing into legalistic Judaism and this book provided key instruction based upon the superiority of Christ Jesus and His finished work on the cross in lieu of ceremonial acts of observance.

Yeshua is superior to the prophets and angels even as the angels are commanded to worship Him as the only Son of Father God. Yeshua, in His timeless message to man reigns timelessly relevant and powerful for today's problems and challenges the Jews of that time and that we Gentiles and Jews in the Diaspora face until He comes again for the church. Yeshua came to us in human form capable of falling to temptation, without ever falling to temptation. In so doing He provided to us an example of life without falling to temptation or compromise. We can claim it is impossible, but a living Jesus faced and won over a greater temptation than I will face, because He communed closely with the Father, which is available to me as well if only I should partake of Him fully.

Israel missed their opportunity for fullest realization of God's blessing because they embraced unbelief; however, we can be redeemed by the blood of the Lamb if only we fully trust in Him. We have the annotation of faith presented in Chapter 11 that we should embrace and emulate even if not especially in this modern age.

Book of the Bible – James
Author – James, the brother of Jesus
Date of Writing – 49 A.D.
Number of Chapters – 5
To Whom Written – Jews in the Diaspora
Purpose of the Writing – To present the model of active and real faith to develop real faith and morals sufficient for real change and growth of character in our Christian lives.

My Personal Summary–

When we worship and study we must worship the authentic God and study the authentic Word of God. It is pointless to worship and study anything less than the Creator and His Word to man. In the first part of James we are given the marks of true religion and thereby, the roadmap to faith.

We are to experience joy in the presence of trials, giving all glory to God. We are to be strong in our faith despite our challenges. We must see the temptations the enemy sets before us and stand or better yet, kneel against them while following Christ who is the source of our blessings and strength. We are told we must flee from evil and subsequent temptation always searching the Truth as a means of pursuing purity and holiness. We are to be gracious and generous to those in need in the Name of Christ.

We are to drive hard after the will of God and inasmuch as we are prone to pre-plan or pre-emote that which we cannot know is what we will be doing a week from now, let alone a year from now. We must do our duty with diligence in the Name of Christ patiently, consistently, humbly, and faithfully.

We are repeatedly reassured/told of the true source of peace, tranquility and healing in the Name of Christ and further, to pray in His Name. We are given so much in the Bible that if only we used on daily basis we would be closer to God, and our brothers and sisters while evangelizing the lost by our words and actions. We would be at that peace we often need, but cannot find. Why can't we find serenity and peace? We don't find the ever-elusive peace because we are most often looking in the lunchmeat drawer for the Bread.

Book of the Bible – 1 Peter
Author – The Apostle Peter
Date of Writing – It is unknown
Number of Chapters – 5
To Whom Written – The elect scattered throughout Asia Minor, Jew and Gentile alike.
Purpose of the Writing – Jesus directly gave Peter two commands: to encourage and strengthen the flock (Luke 22:32) and to feed the flock (John 21:15-17.) This is in compliance with those commands.

My Personal Summary–

"Victory in Jesus, My Savior Forever!"[6] The words of this great hymn echo in my heart, from a little boy worshipping in an old country church sitting next to his faith driven mother, I am now a man worshipping in my study, alone.

A lesson on claiming victory in Christ Jesus is a central theme of this writing of the Apostle Peter. We have victory in the resurrected Christ and we find ourselves instructed to place our hope in the eternal inheritance awaiting we that are saved by grace. We have to stop living as though the hurts, habits and hangups will win... We know the end of His story and we know that He gives us Victory in the end! Today is a great day to be alive! We need to LIVE like it!

Peter reminds us of the price paid for our redemption is the very blood of Yeshua; *"Redeemed by the blood of the Lamb"*[7] we are set on a course

---

[6] Words and Music by E.M. Bartlett© 1939 - Administrated by Integrated Copyright Group, Inc. All rights reserved

[7] "Redeemed" Words by Fanny J. Crosby Music by William J. Kirpatrick 1882

of resolve and perseverance in the living of our lives in a pure and holy and Victorious manner.

Yeshua bore our sins upon the cross so that we could stand firm in the unshakeable foundation of Christ in the midst of fiery challenges and testing in the face of an evil and dark world. Our faith is to transcend the challenges of life that come upon us, as a testimony to those who are lost or weak look upon us to see how we will react to severe battles.

My favorite passage in 1 Peter is:

> *1Pe 2:6 For this is contained in Scripture: "Behold, I lay in Zion a choice stone, a precious corner stone, And he who believes in Him will not be disappointed."*

We will not be disappointed if we believe in Yeshua, the precious cornerstone of our faith. We may not fully understand all that is within the Word of God and His mysteries may remain unknown to us until, through faith we stand before a perfect God to be perfected by His love and presence.

Book of the Bible – 2 Peter
Author – The Apostle Peter
Date of Writing – Between A.D 64 and A.D 70.
Number of Chapters – 3
To Whom Written – Christians everywhere.
Purpose of the Writing – To warn all Christians of the dangers of this world's false teachers and to exhort us to grow in the grace and knowledge of Yeshua.

My Personal Summary–

One of the things I love so much about my alma mater, <u>Master's Divinity School</u> is our emphasis upon the infallible Word of God as the basis for our faith and instruction. In this book Peter warns us of the corrupt teachers waiting to mislead us from the path of obedience and service in the will of God.

There are many *"pulpit pimps"* in our society that preach a *"prosperity doctrine"* that is, while appealing to the contributing masses, are teaching completely contrary to the true Word of God. There are countless examples of preachers occupying opulent mansions, driving exorbitantly luxurious automobiles, and wearing $5,000 custom-made suits while preaching to their struggling congregations the ever attractive *"message of hope"* which requires the people to embrace an entitlement mentality in an atmosphere of whipped-up emotionalism. The truth is absent from these churches, which speak nothing of the cross of neither Christ nor the blood that bought our freedom from sin.

Peter warns us of these who are the false teachers who abound unchecked in our society.

Peter warns us of those that will argue that it has been so long since Jesus was crucified and resurrected that He cannot possibly be returning for His flock because if He were true and real, He would have returned by now. The apostates' goal is to sway faith, dissuade obedience, and turn the faithful from The Source of the faith.

Peter assures the readers of this epistle that Jesus Christ is coming again and that we are to be prepared for His coming through admonitions toward obedience and worship.

Book of the Bible – 1 John
Author – The Apostle John
Date of Writing – Near the end of the first century
Number of Chapters – 5
To Whom Written – The Church in general
Purpose of the Writing – To help guard the Christian church against sin, ward them against false teachers, strengthen their faith in Yeshua and to their joy, assure them of eternal life in Heaven.

My Personal Summary–

This book written by John is a direct and beautiful exhortation toward righteousness and thereby regeneration. We have hope because of Jesus Christ and the gift of the cross and empty grave. John tells us that if we cling to and obey Christ we will be safe from evil. As we see in so many passages written by John, our hope is in Christ and Christ alone. So much so that when Yeshua cleanses this earth of sin on His next coming we who are saved will be like Christ, perfected in His perfection. We will be like Christ when He comes again and though we were saved when on the cross He took away our sins and this time when He comes, He will come with a different purpose for those who have not repented of their sins.

When we live as Yeshua taught and as John emphasized, with love for our brothers we demonstrate the life within us rather than death as sin condemned us. Without Christ we are hopeless and live in fear and desperation clawing out our existence with hate and desperation. In love, through and in Christ Jesus we have a deeper love that transcends cultural and societal differences even though we are all accountable for our unrepentant sins.

When we are obedient to Christ's commandments we live within Christ's love and demonstrate our love for Him through our obedience. Our obedience is a means of worshipping Jesus Christ. We show Jesus is in us when we are obedient showing the world the change a life in Christ can look like.

If we believe in the Name of Christ we shall live eternally in Heaven with Him. We know because of this assurance from Christ and His messenger John.

The Apostle John reminds those who call upon the Name of Christ that in the Name of Christ our prayers are heard and answered. Oh what joy is held in that blessed assurance!

Book of the Bible – 2 John
Author – The Apostle John
Date of Writing – Near the end of the first century
Number of Chapters – 1
To Whom Written – It is apparently the only book of the New Testament written to a woman, and Ephesian matron.
Purpose of the Writing – To warn Christ followers of heretical teaching

My Personal Summary–

The Apostle John tells this dear lady the truth about our Lord and about His commands and promises. We are united in our worship and fellowship in the Name of our Lord for all time because as believers our Lord dwells eternally in the believer. We greet each other in the love and Name of Christ because our church, the gathering of the redeemed is to be a place of holy instruction and brotherly love.

We must obey God and the teachings of Jesus Christ that are timeless and in no way irrelevant as some false prophets would suggest. Because the spirit amongbelievers is to mirror the love of Yeshua we must treat one another with respect. We also must obey because we love Christ and we must walk in the way of the redeemed because to obey is to love.

The sordid error of the world is widespread because there are many who propagate lies against the Name of Christ and His church. They deny the very incarnation of our Lord Jesus Christ, which plainly departs from the true Word. We must guard against these false teachers and preachers who depart from the teaching of Christ. We must not fellowship with those that speak lies against our faith.

The Apostle John expressed his desire to meet with this dear lady in person; however, he could not meet at the local coffee shop, so pen must be put to ink to deliver this message of exhortation and warning. The written Word to mankind, a blessing indeed.

Book of the Bible – 3 John
Author – The Apostle John
Date of Writing – Near the end of the first century
Number of Chapters – 1
To Whom Written – Gaius
Purpose of the Writing – To commend Gaius for his loyalty to the truth and for his care of traveling teachers and missionaries and to recommend Demetrious to Gaius and to warn of his impending visit. In addition he was rebuking Diotrephes for pride.

My Personal Summary–

John speaks from the heart in his delight in knowing Gaius is walking in the Truth, as encouragement for John and Gaius both. This is an important aspect of Christian leadership, mentoring, and Pastoring, to exhort and commend andto compliment and praise publicly. This is leadership in action.

John speaks of supporting such men that walk in the Truth and teach the Truth, which in many aspects of public and private the churches fail miserably in accomplishing in these modern times. Backbiting and divisiveness abound in search of "the faith market share" and ultimately contributors in the seats.

Diotrephes may have sought the favor and accolade of men before the approval of God and His Apostle John. There are many pastors in the world today who are more concerned over being hip, trendy, and cool so that they will be foremost, well-liked. Some have the interest to build legacies that will promote their name forever instead of the Name of Christ, some just want worldly wealth. Conversely there are many pastors who are bigoted, and restrictive on who will enter their church, as though the church is theirs, and not the Lord's.

Many pastors create little personal fiefdoms within "their" churches and they rule them with arrogance and self-centered self-interest without regard for the saving of souls and the honoring of God in their conduct, witness, and preaching.

John would have much rather come in person, but his activities in the Name of Christ and the church would not permit him at that time to visit; however, this letter serves multiple purposes, to commend and to rebuke. John was a master at edifying the body and correcting their wrongs at the same time.

Book of the Bible – Jude
Author – Jude, the brother of James
Date of Writing – Uncertain
Number of Chapters – 1
To Whom Written – Christians who were threatened by apostates and heretics.
Purpose of the Writing – To encourage and warn the Christians to contend for the faith and not be swayed by immoral teaching, heretics and apostates.

My Personal Summary–

Living knowledge of God's Word is a mandate for every Christian, not just pastors. How can we know which way to go lest we have knowledge of our history? How can we avoid pitfalls and traps of the ungodly if we do not know God's history in exposing and punishing those not of God?

Ultimately Jude recounts numerous instances in Biblical history, going all the way back to Enoch in which God took decisive action in rebuking and punishing those that operated from an evil heart falsely claiming to be holy or of God.

Evoking these instances of God's judgments reminds the faithful that God handles the problems within His creation, one way or another, nothing gets by Him. We needn't worry about punishing or vengeance FOR God because God is in charge. However, we do need to be aware of apostates and heretics because they are sneaky, like the serpent they may beguile an immature Christian into diverting, even if only slightly from their true faith.

As in biblical times, so too today will those that mock and blaspheme the Name of Christ and His holy Word be brought to light and punished by a Holy God. We must edify one another while reaching out to the lost while demonstrating our eternal love for God, in whom our eternity is assured.

Jude closes with a benediction of encouragement that points us toward Yeshua, God the Father, and His majesty alone. We are reminded in this elegant closing whom we are to follow, serve, and obey. We follow, serve and obey God and God alone.

Book of the Bible – Revelation
Author – John the Revelator
Date of Writing – A.D. 96
Number of Chapters – 22
To Whom Written – The seven churches of Asia Minor.
Purpose of the Writing – To give hope to Christians, especially those who suffer, by revealing Jesus Christ as the ultimate victorious King of Kings and Lord of Lords. The book manifests its own **AUTHORITY** in declaring itself to be the revelation of Jesus Christ.[8]

My Personal Summary–

One of the most intimidating books of the Bible for most people due to the imagery and dynamic symbolism, Revelation is to me more exciting than the most heralded Hollywood action movie. This book was written by one of the most unique human beings ever to walk the earth, in my opinion. He was so esteemed by God that He chose John to write this

---

[8] Frank Charles Thompson, *Thompson Chain Reference Bible*, (Indianapolis, IN: B. B. Kirkbride Bible Co., 1997), WORD*search* CROSS e-book, Under: "4288, Book of Revelation".

direct revelation of His Word to man telling of Christ's next coming and the installation of God's Heaven for those that are written in the Lamb's Book of Life.

The number seven is written fifty-seven times in Revelation, which could be indicative of completion of God's plan.[9](Seven candlesticks, churches, seals, trumpets, thunders, vials, Spirits, stars. Seven "No mores.")

By contrast, in the completion of His plan we see the elimination of seven things from our world:[10]

Revelation 21:1

No Sorrow

Revelation 21:4

No Crying

Revelation 21:4

No Pain

Revelation 21:4

No Curse

Revelation 22:3

No Night

Revelation 22:5

---

9 Ibid

10 Frank Charles Thompson, "Future," in *Thompson Chain Reference Bible*, (Indianapolis, IN: B. B. Kirkbride Bible Co., 1997), WORD*search* CROSS e-book, Under: "Future".

No Death

Revelation 21:4

No Night

Revelation 22:5

No Death

Revelation 21:4

Make no mistake about it, when Yeshua comes to claim the earth the second time He will not come as a Baby, rather as a conquering King! In the process of wiping this earth clean of sin, He will also end the above seven things during the process of His cleansing.

We as the church are encouraged to read the Word of God because John states the time is near for the return of Christ. In this most apocalyptic book we see extensive symbolism, both literary and idiomatic. We are so fortunate in this the modern technology age because we can read the printed page version of the Word, or we can read the electronic version of the Bible, or we can even listen to an audiobook of the Scriptures! Amazing stuff right? We no longer can plead ignorance because we have so many ways in which we can learn and study God's Word to us.

> The birth of the male child in Revelation 12 is widely regarded as the birth of Jesus Christ. (Revelation 12)

> The sounding of the seventh trumpet is widely heralded as the sound of the victory of Jesus Christ. (Revelation 11:5)

> This is pointedly clear; Jesus Christ is coming again to rescue those that call upon His Name and to condemn forever those that rejected His Name.

Using the Dates of the writing of each Book of the Old and New Testament (as I have already documented above), please enjoy a chart or diagram of the sixty-six (66) Books from the Oldest to the latest (i.e., Genesis – Revelation), noting the date of writing *and the date that the content of the Book actually covers.*

For example, even though Moses wrote the Book of Genesis much later than the actual events, the content of the Book covers the period from Creation to the Egyptian co-mingling. Thus, I arrange the books in the order of actual historical events. This should help you have context time-wise to the events of these times and how they relate to one another.

Next, I list at least three of the major corresponding events of world history next to the Book or collection of Books in any given period (giving only a sentence or short paragraph description for each). For example, the Gospels all cover the exact same historical period (the approximate 33 years of the life and ministry of Jesus), whereas the Book of Genesis covers a vast period of time. An example of major non-Biblical historical events would include the rise of the Chinese dynasties, the rise of the Greek and Roman empires, et al. This I did to help you connect HIStory with history.

Old Testament History Chart[11]

Old Testament History		Secular History
	The dates given reflect the accuracy of modern biblical scholarship, but they should not be regarded as always precise. They are intended to be general guides for Bible students.	Records and dates for early religious and intended history are often incomplete and untrustworthy.
B.C.	**Main Events**	**B.C.**
-2100 **Period of Beginnings**	The Fall The Flood The dispersion of the races	2650 Building of the first pyramids
2092-1877 **Patriarchal Period**	2092 The call of Abraham 1931 Jacob flees from Esau 1886 Joseph becomes Prime Minister of Egypt 1877 Jacob's family enters Egypt	**Oriental Empires**
1877-1382 **Egyptian to Canaan Period**	1806 The death of Joseph 1527 The birth of Moses 1447 The Exodus 1408 Joshua appointed leader 1407 Crossing the Jordan 1407-1382 The conquest of Canaan	1800-1500 **Early Babylonian Empire**
1376-1035 **Judges Period**	1376-1336 Othniel 1197-1157 Gideon 1115-1075 Eli 1075-1035 Samuel For a full list of the Judges see TI#1822	1300-612 **Assyrian Empire**
1051-931 **United Kingdom Period**	1051-1011 Saul 1011-971 David 971-931 Solomon 960 Dedication of the Temple	

---

[11] Frank Charles Thompson, *Thompson Chain Reference Bible*, (Indianapolis, IN: B. B. Kirkbride Bible Co., 1997), WORD*search* CROSS e-book, Under: "4222b, Old Testament History Chart".

	Kingdom of	Kingdom of	Prophets	753 Rome
931-587/6 Divided Kingdom Period	**Israel** 931 Jeroboam 722 Hoshea 722 The captivity of Israel	**Judah** 931 Rehoboam 587/6 Zedekiah 587/6 The captivity of Judah	875-800 Elijah, Elisha 841-810 Obadiah, Joel 782-725 Jonah, Hosea 758-730 Amos, Micah 739-620 Isaiah, Nahum 621-609 Habakkuk 636-623 Zephaniah 627-560 Jeremiah, Ezekiel	founded 745 Later Assyrian Empire 732 Damascus falls
	For a full list of the kings see 1823, 1824		605-505 Daniel, Haggai 520-489 Zechariah 430 Malachi	612-539 **Babylonian Empire** 539 Babylon captured by Cyrus
587/6-331 Post-Exilic and Persian Period	536 Jews return under Zerubbabel 516 The temple dedicated 458 Ezra leads back a caravan of Jews 445 Nehemiah returns to Jerusalem and begins to repair the city walls			539-331 **Persian Empire**

Interval Between the Testaments (*see also* 4219a)	**Secular History**
B.C. - A.D. **Main Events**	
331- 166 B.C. Greek and Egyptian Period 320 B.C. Judea annexed to Egypt	330 B.C. Final conquest by Alexander the Great 330-166 B.C. Kingdom of Alexander's Successors
193 B.C. Judea annexed to Syria	

166 B.C. -	166-63 B.C. Jewish independence under the Maccabees	63 B.C.
63 B.C.	168 B.C. Antiochus pollutes the temple	Pompey, the
Maccabean	167 B.C. Beginning of the Maccabaean revolt	Roman general
Period	165 B.C. The temple is rededicated	captured
		Jerusalem and
		from this time
		the provinces of
		Palestine were
		subject to Rome

New Testament History

Roman Emperors

63 B.C. -	The portion of the chart below gives the names of the
166 B.C.	provinces, the rulers and approximate dates of their
Roman	rulership, and also a few outstanding events The local
Period	government was entrusted part of the time to princes who
(Time of	had political influence at Rome, and at other periods to
Herods)	procurators appointed by the emperors.

37 B.C. - A.D. 4

Herod the Great was king of Judea. In the time of Augustus his realm was enlarged to include a considerable territory east of the Jordan. At the time of Christ's birth he was the ruler of all Palestine. He probably died the same year that Christ was born, and his province was divided between his sons.

27 B.C. - 14 A.D. Augustus Caesar

Judea (Judea and Samaria)	**Galilee** and **Perea**	Fifth Province (Country east of Galilee)		
4 B.C. - A.D. 6 **Archelaus** Ethnarch	B.C. 4 - 39 A.D. **Herod Antipas** Tetrarch	B.C. 4 - A.D. 33 **Herod Phillip** Tetrarch	4 B.C.—Birth of Christ 2 B.C. (?)— Birth of Paul A.D. 25-27 (?)—Baptism of Christ	A.D. 14-37 Tiberius Caesar
A.D. 26-36 **Pontius Pilate** Procurator			A.D. 29-30 (?)—Crucifixion A.D. 31- 37 (?)— Conversion of Paul	
A.D. 39-44 **Herod Agrippa I**, King of the whole country (procurators from A.D. 44-52)				A.D. 37-41 Caligula
A.D. 52-58 **Felix** Procurator			A.D. 45-58 (?) **Paul's** Missionary journeys	A.D. 41-54 Claudius

A.D. 58-61 (?) Festus Procurator	A.D. 48-70 **Herod Agrippa II** king of Chalcis and other adjacent regions	A.D. 61-68 (?) Paul's one or two (?) imprisonments at Rome	A.D. 68-69 Galba, Otho, Vitellius
	King of Chalcis A.D. 48-53 Area expanded to the South A.D. 53 Area expanded to include Galilee A.D. 61	A.D. 70 End of the Jewish state. Jerusalem destroyed by Titus.	A.D. 69-79 Vespasian
		A.D. 90-100 Persecution of Christians by Domitian. Death of John and close of apostolic age.	A.D. 79-81 Titus A.D. 81-98 Domitian

Chronological Old Testament[12]

The Old Testament is a collection of thirty-nine books. They were written to disclose the Covenant God of Israel as he revealed himself and how he acts toward his children. From its beginning pages the Old Testament presents itself to the reader as a book that describes the relationship of God and his people. It is not known with precision when the Old Testament was first assembled into one volume. The first section of the Old Testament often called the Law was canonized (accepted as divinely inspired and authorized) between 450-300 B.C. The Prophets, another section of similar books, were received as canon about 200 B.C. The Writings, largely the poetry book, were accepted sometime in the second century B.C. One must remember that the faith of Israel existed independently of any inspired books for hundreds of years. This should give us pause to bear in mind that we can worship the God of the Bible without having to worship Scripture itself.

This does not mean that Scripture is not important in the daily expression of our Christian life. It does mean that we should remember

---

[12] http://www.sbl.org/readthrubible/chronological/ot/index.shtm

that Scripture is God's tool to express how he will act toward us in our life situations.

It is a means to an end, not the end in itself. This is not to say that Scripture is not important. It is saying that the God of Scripture is more important than the words of Scripture.

Creation Stage (Genesis 1.1-11.26) Dates Covered: 2150B.C.-1406B.C. Secular Events: 1. earliest form of writing – Cuneiform c.3200. 2. The city of Ur Falls c.2004. 3. The Law code of Hammurapi c.1972-1750B.C.

Creation
- Creation of the Universe: Gen 1.1-2.4a
- Creation of Adam and Eve: Gen 2.4b-25

Fall
- Forbidden Fruit: Gen 3.1-24
- The Killing Field: Gen 4.1-16

Flood
- The Daughters of Men: Gen 6.1-8
- Building and Floating: Gen 6.9-8.22
- Noah Begins Again: Gen 9.1-28
- The Descendants of Noah: Gen 10.1-32

Babel/Nations
- Going Higher and Loosing Communication: Gen 11.1-9

Patriarchal Stage (Job 1.1-42.17; Genesis 12.1-50.26)
- The Suffering of Job: Job 1.1-2.13
- Job's Opening Speech: Job 3.1-26
- Job's Friends: Job 4.1-27.23
- Wisdom: Job 28.1-28
- Final Summation: Job 29.1-37.24
- Job's Closing Speech: Job 38.1-42.6
- Job's Suffering Reversed: Job 42.7-17

Abraham: (the Promise of a Son): Genesis 11.27-20.18

- The Journey to Canaan and Egypt (Promise of Descendants and Land): Gen 11.27-12-20
- Abraham and Lot (Separation and Rescue): Gen 13.1-14.24
- The Promise of God to Abraham: Gen 15.1-21
- Hagar and Ishmael: Gen 16.1-16
- God's Covenant with Abraham (Name changed, circumcision instituted, promise of a son given again, Abraham and Ishmael circumcised) Gen 17.1-27
- The Promise of God for a Son (Sarah laughs): Gen 18.1-15
- Abraham, Lot, Sodom and Gomorrah: Gen 18.16-19.38
- Abraham and Abimelech (Abraham lies about Sarah in Gerar and God protects her): Gen 20.1-18

Isaac (Strife between Older and Younger Brothers): Genesis 21.1-27.40

- The Birth of Isaac: Gen 21.1-7
- Hagar and Ishmael: Gen 21.8-21
- Abraham Offers Isaac to God: Gen 22.1-19
- Sarah's Death: Gen 23.1-20
- Isaac and Rebekah: Gen 24.1-67
- Abraham Dies: Gen 25.1-10
- Jacob and Esau's Birth: Gen 25.19-34
- Strife over Abraham's Wells: Gen 26.1-33
- God Chooses Jacob: Gen 27.1-40

Jacob: (Exile and God's Protection and Blessing): Genesis 27.41-37.1

- Jacob Flees to Laban: Gen 27.41-28.9
- Jacob's Dream at Bethel: Gen 28.10-22
- Jacob's Marriage: Gen 29.1-30.24
- Jacob's First Scheme: Gen 30.25-43
- Jacob and Laban: Gen 31.1-55
- Jacob Prepares to Meet Esau, wrestles with God, meets Esau: Gen 32.1-33.20
- Dinah and the Shechemites: Gen 34.1-31
- Returning to Bethel: Gen 35.1-15
- The Death of Rachel and Isaac: Gen 35.16-29

Joseph (Relationship with Brothers): Genesis 37.2-50.26
- Joseph the Dreamer (sold by his brothers): Gen 37.2-36
- Judah and Tamar: Gen 38.1-30
- The Wife of Potiphar: Gen 39.1-23
- Joseph Interprets Dreams: Gen 40.1-41.57
- The Brother's of Joseph Journey to Egypt: Gen 42.1-47.12
- Joseph Ascends in Egypt: Gen 47.13-31
- Manasseh, Ephraim: Gen 48.1-22
- Jacob Blesses his Sons and Dies: Gen 49.1-50.14
- Joseph Reassures his brothers and dies: Gen 50.15-26

Exodus Stage (Exodus 1.1-19.2)
Exodus from Egypt: 1.1-13.16
- Israel Oppressed and the Birth of Moses: Ex 1.1-2.10
- Moses Leaves Israel: Ex 2.11-25
- Moses meets God: Ex 3.1-4.17
- Moses Returns to Egypt: Ex 4.18-31
- Moses and Pharaoh: Ex 5.1-7.13
- Plagues in Egypt: Ex 7.14-11.10
- The Passover and Redemption: Ex 12.1-13.16

Journey into the Wilderness: 13.17-19.2
- Departure from Egypt: Ex 13.17-15.27
- Water, Manna, and Quail: Ex 15.22-17.7
- Amalekites and Arrival: 18.1-19.2

Covenant Stage (Exodus 19.3-Deuteronomy 34.12)
The Lord-Servant Treaty (Exodus 19.3-Numbers 10.10

This section of the Pentateuch is self-contained at describes some of the teachings that Israel needed on their way to the promise land. It covers the period from Israel's arrival at Mt. Sinai (Exodus 19.3) to their departure (Numbers 10.10). The time period is about one year in the life of Israel.

- Theophany on Sinai: 19.3-20.21 (10 commandments 20.1-17)
- God has no form: 20.22-24.11 (judicial laws: 21.1-23.33)

- Instructions for building Tabernacle and dedicating priest: 24.12-18-34.28 (laws given: 25.2-31.17)
- Tabernacle building: 34.29-40.28 (laws followed 35.1-40.33) Regulations about Sacrifices: Leviticus 1-10 [Regulations about Purity: 11-18] Sacrificial laws and priest dedication: Lev. 1-10 (laws of sacrifice (1.2-9.24; purity laws 11-18)
- Marching orders: Lev. 19.1-Num. 10.10 (holiness laws (Lev 19.4-Num 9.14; marching orders: Num. 9.15-10.10)

Journey to the Promised Land (Numbers 10.11-Deuteronomy 34)
Wilderness Journey: 10.11-21.20
- Leaving Sinai and Complaining: Num 10.11-11-35
- God's Punishment of Miriam and Aaron: Num 12.1-16
- Kadesh Rebellion: Num 13.1-14.45 [Regulations: Num 15.1-36]
- Korah's Revolt: Num 15.37-16.50
- Aaron: Num 17.1-18.32
- Kadesh Rebellion: Num 20.1-21
- Aaron's Death, Complaining, Arrival at Moab: 20.22-21.20

Victory in Moab: Numbers 21.21-Deuteronomy 3.29
- From Sihon to Sihon: Num 21.21-Deut 2.3.29 [Obey God: Deut 4-11 An Exhortation to Israel to obey God] [Various Stipulations: Deut 12-26 Stipulations to keep in the new land]

Moses' Final Words: Deut 27-34
- Moses gives final Instructions: 29.1-20
- Joshua and the twelve tribes: 31.1-33.29
- The Death of Moses: 34.1-12

Conquest Stage (Joshua 1-24)
The Conquest of Canaan: Joshua 1-12
- Joshua becomes Israel's Leader: Joshua 1.1-18
- Rahab hides spies: Joshua 2.1-24

- Crossing into the Promised Land: Joshua 3.1-5.12
- Walls of Jericho fall down: Joshua 5.13-6.27
- Achan's Sin: Joshua 7.1-8.29
- Covenant and Deception: Joshua 8.30-9.27
- War in Canaan: Joshua 10.1-11-23
  [List of conquered kings: 12.1-24]
- God's challenge to Joshua: 13.1-7
  [Allocation of Land: 13.8-22.34]
- Me and my house: 23.1-24.33

Judges Stage (Judges 1-24; Ruth 1-4)
- Israel's forgets God (theological explanation): Judges 1.1-3.6

The Judges: Judges 3.7-16.31
- Othniel and Ehud: Judges 3.7-30
- Deborah and Barak: Judges 4.1-5.31
- Gideon: Judges 6.1-8.32
- Abimelech: Judges 8.33-9.57
- Jephthah: Judges 10.6-12.7
- Samson: Judges 13.1-16.31

Various Concluding Stories: Judges 17-21
- The grandson of Moses runs an idolatrous cult in Dan Judges: 17-19
- The rape of a concubine and a war of retribution: Judges 19-21

Ruth (Ruth 1-4)
- Family lose, Ruth's conversion and arrival in Bethlehem: Ruth 1.1-22
- Ruth and Boaz meet: Ruth 2.1-23
- Ruth's proposal to Boaz: Ruth 3.1-18
- Kinsman-Redeemer: Ruth 4.1-22

United Kingdom Stage (1 Samuel 1.1-1 Kings 11.43)
Samuel (1 Samuel 1-7)
- The Birth of Samuel (Hannah's Prayer): 1 Sam 1.1-2.11
- The Wicked Sons of Eli: 1 Sam 2.12-2.36

- The Call of Samuel by God: 1 Sam 3.1-4.1a
- The Ark is Lost: 1 Sam 4.1-7.1
- Samuel Rules: 1 Sam 7.2-17

Saul (1 Samuel 8-15)
- Saul Becomes King: 1 Sam 8.1-11.15
- Samuel says Goodbye: 1 Sam 12.1-25
- The Philistines: 1 Sam 13.1-14.52
- God Rejects Saul: 1 Sam 15.1-35

David (1 Samuel 16-1. 1 Kings 2.12)
- David anointed and serves Saul: 1 Sam 16.1-23
- David and Goliath: 1 Sam 17.1-58
- David on the Run (Success and Jealousy): 1 Sam 18.1-27.12
  [Psalm 11: Possibly set against 1 Sam 18.8-19.7]
  [Psalm 7: Possibly set against 1 Sam 18.10-24]
  [Psalm 59: David's prays for God's strength as Solomon chases him 1 Sam 19.10-11]
  [Psalm 57: When David had fled from Saul into the cave 1 Sam 21]
  [Psalm 142: When David had fled from Saul into the cave 1 Sam 21]
  [Psalm 34: Set against 1 Samuel 21]
  [Psalm 56: Set against 1 Samuel 21.1015]
  [Psalm 17: Possibly set against 1 Sam 23.25ff.]
- Saul and the spirit of Samuel (the witch at Endor): 1 Kings 28.1-25
- Saul and his sons die: 1 Sam 29.1-31.13
- David, Saul's Killer, Laments: 2 Sam 1.1-27
- David the King of Judah: 2 Sam 2.1-4.12
- David the King of Israel (philistines and dancing before God: 2 Sam 5.1-6.23
  [Psalm 24: Set against 2 Samuel 6 (the restoration of the ark)]
  [Psalm 68: Set against 2 Samuel 6.12-16]
- God's Covenant with David and his Response: 2 Sam 7.1-29

[Psalm 2: Rooted in 2 Samuel 7, the promise to David of a supreme name]
- David the Warrior: 2 Sam 8.1-10.19
- David and Bathsheba: 2 Sam 11.1-27
- Nathan's Rebuke of David's Sin: 2 Sam 12.1-31
  [Psalm 51: David's Repentance of the Bathsheba Affair]
- The Consequences of David's Sin: 2 Sam 13.1-20.26
  [Psalm 3: Set against 2 Sam 15.13-17.24]
  [Psalm 4: Set against David's fleeing from Absalom]
  [Psalm 5: Set against David's fleeing from Absalom]
  [Psalm 6: Set against David's fleeing from Absalom]
  [Psalm 63: Set against David's fleeing from Absalom]
- David's Rule Ends: 2 Sam 2 Sam 21.1-1 Kings 2.12

Solomon (1 Kings 2.13-11.43)
- Solomon Becomes King: 1 Kings 2.13-46
- Solomon's Wisdom: 1 Kings 3.1-28
  [Government Overview: 1 Kings 4.1-28]
- The Temple for God: 1 Kings 5.1-9.9
- Government Overview: 1 Kings 9.15-28]
- The Queen of Sheba and Great Wealth: 1 Kings 10.1-29
- Solomon Breaks Covenant (marriage to foreign women): 1 Kings 11.1-43
  [Proverbs: A collection of practical bits of Wisdom by Solomon and others]
  [The Song of Songs: May or may not be by Solomon, A poetic portrayal of the reomatic relationship between a young man and a young woman]
  [Ecclesiastes: Addresses the issue of the meaning of Live: may or may not be by Solomon]

Divided Kingdom Stage (1 Kings 12.1-2 Kings 25.30)
Northern Kingdom (1ˢᵗ seven kings): 1 Kings12.1-16.34
- Rehoboam, Jeroboam, and the Splitting of the Kingdom: 1 Kings 12.1-24
- Jeroboam (N): 1 Kings 12.25-14-20

- Three Judean Kings (Jeroboam, Abijah, Asa [S]): 14.21-15.24
- Nadab, Baasha, Elah, Zimri, Omri, Ahab (N): 1 Kings 15.2516.34

Elijah Stories: 1 Kings 17.1-2 Kings 2.12a
- Elijah and Ahab: 17.1-18.46
- God encourages Elijah: 19.1-21
  [Israel and Aram at war: 22.1-40]
- Naboth's vineyard: 21.1-29
- Jehoshaphat: 22.41-50
  [Psalm 83: Set against the reign of Jehoshaphat (2 Chronicles 20)]
- Elijah and Ahaziah: 1 Kings 22.51-2 Kings 1.18
- Elijah goes to heaven: 2 Kings 2.1-12a

Elisha Stories: 2 Kings 2.12b-8.6
- The Company of Prophets: 2 Kings 12b-18
- Water, Mocking, Water. Poison, Loaves: 2 Kings 2.19-4.44
- Naaman Healed: 2 Kings 5.1-27
- Axhead, Blinding, Provision, Healing: 2 Kings 6.1-8.6

More Kings: 2 Kings 8.7-13.35
- Elisha and Hazael: 2 Kings 8.7-15
- Jehoram and Ahaziah (S): 2 Kings 8.16-29
- Jehu and the Death of Jezebel and Ahab (N): 2 Kings 9.1-10.35
- Joash (S): 2 Kings 11.1-12.21
  [Joel (Southern Prophet) A prophesy against Judah: Joel 1.1-3.21]
- Jehoahez and Jehoash (N): 2 Kings 13.1-35

[Jonah (Northern Prophet) Prophecy to Ninevah]
- God's Call, Jonah's Response: 1.1-17
- From the Fish: Jonah 2.1-10
- God Calls Again: 3.1-10
- Jonah's Resentment: 4.1-11

Northern Kingdom (final years): 2 Kings 14.1-17.41
- Amaziah (S): 2 Kings 14.1-22

[Joel (Southern Prophet) A prophesy against Judah: Joel 1.1-3.21]
- Jeroboam II (N) 14.23-29
[Amos (Northern Prophet) A prophesy against Israel: Amos 1.1-9.15]
- Uzziah (Judah): 15.1-7
[Isaiah and Micah (Southern Prophets) Prophecies against Judah]
- Zechariah, Shallum, Menahem, Pekahiah Pekah: (N): 2 Kings 15.8-31
[Hosea (Northern Prophet) A prophesy against Israel (N): Hosea 1.1-14.9]
- Jotham and Ahaz (S): 2 Kings 15.32-16.20
[Isaiah and Micah (Southern Prophets) Prophecies against Judah]
- Hoshea (fall of northern kingdom): 17.1-41
[Hosea (Northern Prophet) A prophesy against Israel (N): Hosea 1.1-14.9]

Southern Kingdom (final years): 2 Kings 18.1-25.30
- Hezekiah (S): 18.1-20.21
[Psalm 75: Set against 2 Kings 18-19]
[Psalm 76: Set against 2 Kings 18-19]
[Isaiah and Micah (Southern Prophets) Prophecies against Judah]
- Manasseh: 21.1-18
- Amon (S): 21.19-26
[Nahum and Zephaniah (Southern Prophets) Prophecies against Judah]
- Josiah, Jehoahaz, Johoiakim, Jehoiachin (S): 22.1-24.18
[Jeremiah (Southern Prophets) Prophecies against Judah]
- Zedekiah (S): 24.18-25.30
[Psalm 74: Set against the events of 2 Kings 24-25]
[Jeremiah and Ezekiel (Southern Prophets) Prophecies against Judah]

[Habakkuk (Southern Prophet) The just live because of the Faithfulness of God]

Captivity (not covered by any one book)

[Jeremiah and Ezekiel (Southern Prophets) Prophecies in Exile]
[Lamentations: A eulogy of mourning of the fall of Jerusalem in 586 B.C.

Daniel (1-6)

- Daniel and his three friends: 1
- Nebuchadnezzar's dream: 2
- Fiery furnace: 3
- Nebuchadnezzar's insanity: 4
- Handwriting on the wall: 5
- The lions' den: 6
  [Obadiah (Exile Prophet) Edom's mistreatment of Judeans during the Babylonia destruction of Jerusalem]

Restoration (Ezra; Nehemiah; Esther)

Ezra

- Zerubbabel Return and Temple Building Begins: Ezra 1.1-4-24
- Prophets Encouragement: 5.1-12
  [Haggai and Zechariah (Restoration Prophets) Prophecies about building the Temple]
- Temple Completed: Ezra 3-6.22
- Ezra Returns: Ezra 7.1-8.22
  [List of people: 7.27-8.21]
- Ezra's deals with intermarriage: Ezra 9-10

Nehemiah

- Nehemiah's Return: Nehemiah 1-2
- Rebuilding Walls, Opposition, Plot: 3.1-4.23
- Helping Poor, Plot, Opposition, Walls Completed: 5.1-7.3
  [List of returnees; 7.4-73]
- Ezra assembles people, Reforms: Nehemiah 8.1-10.39
  [List of names: 11.1-36]

- Nehemiah assembles People, Reforms: Nehemiah 12.27-13.31
  [Malachi (Restoration Prophet) Prophecies about robbing God]
  [1 and 2 Chronicles: A retelling spin of the story of 1 & 2 Kings
  for the sake of the people of the restoration]

Esther
- The King and the Queen: Esther 1.1-2.23
- Haman's and Mordecai: Esther 3.1-4.17
- Esther's Banquets: 5.1-7.10
- Haman's Plot Foiled, Jews Saved: Esther 8.1-9.10
- Esther, Susa, Feast of Purim: 9.11-10.3

Chronological New Testament

The New Testament was written over a sixty-year period in the first century. While Jesus lived at the beginning of the first century (6 B.C. - A.D. 33), the Gospels that tell his story were not written until later and then they were not the first books written.

Paul was the first one to write what we call a New Testament book. Most likely it was written after his first journey around the Asia. After he returned, he spent some considerable time at Antioch in Syria (Acts 14.28) sharing what God had accomplished on their journey. From Antioch in Syria, he penned his first letter, which is our book of Galatians. Below is the chronological arrangement of the New Testament.

Galatians: Christian Freedom

Opening Thoughts: 1.1-5
    Faithfulness to One Gospel: An Autobiography 1.6-2.21
    Faithfulness to One Gospel: A Rebuke 3.1-4.31
    Faithfulness to One Gospel: A Request 5.1-6.10
Closing Thoughts: 6.11-18

James: Faith at Work

Opening Thought: 1.1
>True Religion 1.2-18
>True Worship 1.19-27
>True Faith 2.1-26
>True Wisdom 3.1-5.20

1 Thessalonians: He's is Coming

Opening Thought: 1.1
>In Suffering Become Imitators 1.2-10
>Imitation of Paul's Ministry 2.1-4.12
>Instruction about the Second Coming 4.13-5.24

Closing Thoughts 5.25-28

2 Thessalonians: The Day of the Lord

Opening Thoughts: 1.1-2
>Encouragement during Suffering 1.3-12
>Enlightenment about Christ's Return 2.1-17
>Exhortation to Steadfastness 3.1-15

Closing Thoughts: 3.16-18

1 Corinthians: Problem Solving

Opening Thoughts: 1.1-3
>Admonition Concerning Divisions 1.4-4.20
>Activities Denounced 5.1-6.20
>Answers to Corinthian Questions 7.1-16.9

Closing Thoughts: 16.10-24

2 Corinthians: Reconciliation

Opening Thoughts: 1.1-2
    Devoted Majority 1.3-7.16
    Deliverance for Jerusalem Saints 8.1-9.15
    Disobedient Minority 10.1-13.10
Closing Thoughts 13.11-14

Romans: God's Righteousness

Opening Thoughts: 1.1-17
    Slave to Sin 1.18-3.20
    Slave to God 3.21-8.39
    Salvation of Israel 9.1-11.36
    Service to God 12.1-16.24
Closing Thoughts: 16.25-27

Mark: An Evangelistic Tract

    Preparation of Jesus 1.1-13
    Presentation of Jesus 1.14-8.30
    Passion of Jesus 8.31-16.8

Philemon: An Appeal for Forgiveness

Opening Thoughts 1-3
    Approval of Philemon 4-7
    Appeal to Philemon 8-14
    Assurance for Philemon 15-22
Closing Thoughts: 23-25

Colossians: How to Deal With Cults

Opening Thoughts:1.1-14
   True Christian Doctrine 1.15-2.23
   True Christian Deportment 3.1-4.6
Closing Thoughts: 4.7-18

Ephesians: The Church

Opening Thoughts: 1.1-3
   Purpose and Plan of God 1.4-23
   Purpose Demonstrated in the Church 2.1-22
   Purpose Demonstrated in Paul 3.1-21
   Purpose Lived Out in Community 4.1-6.20
Closing Thoughts: 6.21.24

Luke: A Defense of the Gospel of Jesus

Opening Thoughts: 1.1-4
   Life of Jesus - Early accounts 1.5-4.13
   Upper Galilean Ministry 4.14-9.50
   Keen Determination of Jesus 9.51-19.27
   Execution of Jesus 19.28-24.53

Acts: A Defense of the Ministry of Paul

Spirit Arrives in Jerusalem 1.1-6.7
   Proclamation in Judea-Samaria 6.8-9.31
   Inclusion of Gentiles 9.32-12.25
   Received Gospel in Asia 13.1-16.5
   Involvement of Gospel in Asia 16.6-19.20
   Trials - Appeal - Rome 19.21-28.31

Philippians: Joy Comes When Unity Abides

Opening Thoughts: 1.1-2
    Paul's Interest in the Philippian Church 1.3-26
    An Exhortation: The Pattern Of Christ to Follow 1.27-2.18
    Example of Timothy 2.19-24
    Example of Epaphroditus 2.25-30
    An Exhortation: The Pattern of Paul to Follow 3.1-4.9
    Philippian Church's Interest in Paul 4.10-20
Closing Thoughts: 4.21-23

1 Timothy: Pastoring A Second Generation Church

Opening Thoughts: 1.1-2
    Teach Sound Doctrine 1.3-20
    Edict for Public Worship 2.1-15
    Administration - Elders - Deacons 3.1-16
    Combat False Teachers 4.1-16
    Hints on Widows, Elders, and Slaves 5.1-6.3
Closing Thoughts: 6.3-21

Titus: Pastoring a First Generation Church

Opening Thoughts: 1.1-4
    Appointment of Elders 1.5-9
    Against False Teachers 1.10-16
    Advice on Practical Living 2.1-3.11
Closing Thoughts: 3.12-15

2 Timothy: Passing the Torch!

Opening Thoughts 1.1-2
    Petition for Courage 1.3-2.13
    Pastoral Responsibilities 2.14-4.5

Paul's Final Words 4.6-18
Closing Thoughts: 4.19-22

1 Peter: What to Do When The Hard Time Comes

Opening Thoughts: 1.1-2
  Praise to God 1.3-12
  Exhortation to Holy Living 1.13-21
  Toward Mutual Love 1.22-25
  Elevation to God's People 2.1-25
  Responsibilities of Believers 3.1-5.11
Closing Thoughts: 5.12-14

2 Peter: What Do You Mean He's Not Coming?

Opening Thoughts: 1.1-2
  True Knowledge 1.3-21
  Warning Against False Teachers 2.1-22
  Obsolete Doctrine No! 3.1-18

Matthew: How To Teach New Converts

Birth And Infancy : 1-2
Book One
  Narrative. Teaching, Healing and Preaching: 3.1-4.25
  Instruction. Sermon On The Mount: 5-7

Book Two
  Narrative. The Works Of The Kingdom: 8.1-9.38
  Instruction. The Disciples Sent Out: 10.1-11.1

Book Three
  Narrative. What The Kingdom Is Not: 11.2-12.50
  Instruction. The Parables Of The Kingdom: 13.1-53

Book Four
Narrative. Suffering, Miracles, Conflict: 13.54-17.27
Instruction. Humility, Forgiveness: 18.1-35

Book Five
Narrative. The Old Age and The Age To Come: 19.1-23.39
Instruction. The Future Kingdom: 24-25
Death, Resurrection, Instructions : 26-28

Hebrews: A First Century Sermon

Christ ...
Superior to the Prophets 1.1-3
Superior to the Angels 1.4-2.18
Superior to Moses-Joshua 3.1-4.13
Superior to the Priesthood 4.14-7.28
Superior Covenant 8.1-10.18
Faith ...
Superior Way 10.19-12.29
Closing Thoughts: 13.1-25

Jude: Combat Ready!

Opening Thoughs:1-2
Contend for the Faith: Why? 3-16
Contend for the Faith: How? 17-23
Closing Thoughts: 24-25

2 John: Undesirable Guest

Opening Thoughts: 1-3
Love One Another 4-6
Look Out For Error 7-11
Closing Thoughts: 12-13

1 John: Belief Problems With A New Generation

Complete Joy 1.1-4
    Conduct 1.5-2.6
    Christian Love 2.7-17
    Christ in Believer 2.18-28
    Conduct 2.29-3.10
    Christian Love 3.11-24
    Christ in Believer 4.1-6
    Christian Love 4.7-5.12
    Conduct 5.13-21

3 John: Church Discipline is Important

Opening Thought: 1
    Service of Gaius 2-8
    Strife of Diotrephes 9-12
Closing Thoughts: 13-14

John: So That You May Continue To Believe

Opening Thoughts: 1.1-18
    Public Ministry of Jesus 1.19-12.50
    Private Ministry of Jesus 13.1-17.26
    Passover, Crucifixion, Resurrection 18.1-20.31
Closing Thoughts: 21.1-25

Revelation: A Book of Comfort – Dates Covered: 8 B.C. - A.D. 96. 1. Mount Vesuvius Erupts A.D. 79. 2. Claudius conquers Britain for Rome A.D. 43. 3. Construction begins on Roman Coliseum A.D. 71.

Opening Thoughts: 1.1-8
    Vision One 1.9-3.22
    Vision Two 4.1-16.21
    Interlude One 7.1-17

Interlude Two 10.1-11.13
Interlude Three 12.1-14.20
Vision Three 17.1-21.8
Vision Four 21.9-22.5
Closing Thoughts: 22.6-21

Dates Covered: 2150B.C.-1406B.C. Secular Events: 1. earliest form of writing – Cuneiformc.3200. 2. The city of Ur Falls c.2004. 3. The Law code of Hammurapi c.1972-1750B.C. Genesis 1-3 Genesis 4-7 Genesis 8-11 Job 1-5 Job 6-9 Job 10-13 Job 14-16	Job 17-20 Job 21-23 Job 24-28 Job 29-31 Job 32-34 Job 35-37 Job 38-39	Job 40-42 Genesis 12-15 Genesis 16-18 Genesis 19-21 Genesis 22-24 Genesis 25-26 Genesis 27-29	Genesis 30-31 Genesis 32-34 Genesis 35-37 Genesis 38-40 Genesis 41-42 Genesis 43-45 Genesis 46-47	Genesis 48-50 Exodus 1-3 Exodus 4-6 Exodus 7-9 Exodus 10-12 Exodus 13-15 Exodus 16-18

Exodus 19-21 Exodus 22-24 Exodus 25-27 Exodus 28-29 Exodus 30-32 Exodus 33-35 Exodus 36-38	Exodus 39-40 Leviticus 1-4 Leviticus 5-7 Leviticus 8-10 Leviticus 11-13 Leviticus 14-15 Leviticus 16-18	Leviticus 19-21 Leviticus 22-23 Leviticus 24-25 Leviticus 26-27 Numbers 1-2 Numbers 3-4 Numbers 5-6	Numbers 7 Numbers 8-12 Numbers 11-13 Numbers 14-15 & Psalm 90 Numbers 16-17 Numbers 18-20 Numbers 21-22	Numbers 23-25 Numbers 26-27 Numbers 28-30 Numbers 31-32 Numbers 33-34 Numbers 35-36 Deuteronomy 1-2

Deuteronomy 3-4 Deuteronomy 5-7 Deuteronomy 8-10 Deuteronomy 11-13 Deuteronomy 14-16 Deuteronomy 17-20 Deuteronomy 21-23	Deuteronomy 24-27 Deuteronomy 28-29 Deuteronomy 30-31 Deuteronomy 32-34 & Psalm 91* Joshua 1-4 Joshua 5-8 Joshua 9-11	Joshua 12-15 Joshua 16-18 Joshua 19-21 Joshua 22-24 Judges 1-2 Judges 3-5 Judges 6-7	Judges 8-9 Judges 10-12 Judges 13-15 Judges 16-18 Judges 19-21 Ruth 1 Samuel 1-3	1 Samuel 4-8 1 Samuel 9-12 1 Samuel 13-14 1 Samuel 15-17 1 Samuel 18-20 & Psalm 11 and 59 1 Samuel 21-24 Psalms 7, 27, 31, 34, 52

Psalms 56, 120, 140-142 1 Samuel 25-27 Psalms 17, 35, 54, 63 1 Samuel 28-31; Psalms 18; 1 Chronicles 10 Psalms 121, 123-125, 128-130 2 Samuel 1-4 Psalms 6, 8-10, 14, 16, 19, 21	1 Chronicles 1-2 Psalms 43-45, 49, 84-85, 87 1 Chronicles 3-5 Psalms 73, 77-78 1 Chronicles 6 Psalms 81, 88, 92-93 1 Chronicles 7-10	Psalms 102-104 2 Samuel 5:10; 1 Chronicles 11-12 Psalm 133 Psalms 106-107 2 Samuel 5:11-6:23; 1 Chronicles 13-16 Psalms 1-2, 15, 22-24, 47, 68 Psalms 89, 96, 100-101, 105, 132	2 Samuel 7; 1 Chronicles 17 Psalms 25, 29, 33, 36, 39 2 Samuel 8-9; 1 Chronicles 18 Psalms 50, 53, 60, 75 2 Samuel 10; 1 Chronicles 19; Psalms 20 Psalms 65-67, 69-70 2 Samuel 11-12; 1 Chronicles 20	Psalms 32, 51, 86, 122 2 Samuel 13-15 Psalms 3-4, 12-13, 28, 55 2 Samuel 16-18 Psalms 26, 40, 58, 61, 62, 64 2 Samuel 19-21 Psalms 5, 38, 41, 42

2 Samuel 22-23, 57 Psalms 95, 97-99 2 Samuel 24; 1 Chronicles 21-22; Psalms 30 Psalms 108-110 1 Chronicles 23-25 Psalms 131, 138, 139, 143-145 1 Chronicles 26-29; Psalms 127	Psalms 111-118 1 Kings 1-2; Psalms 37, 71, 94 Psalms 119:1-88 1 Kings 3-4; 2 Chronicles 1; Psalms 72 Psalms 119:89-176 Song of Solomon Proverbs 1-3	Proverbs 4-6 Proverbs 7-9 Proverbs 10-12 Proverbs 13-15 Proverbs 16-18 Proverbs 19-21 Proverbs 22-24	1 Kings 5-6; 2 Chronicles 2-3 1 Kings 7; 2 Chronicles 4 1 Kings 8; 2 Chronicles 5 2 Chronicles 6-7; Psalms 136 Psalms 134, 146-150 1 Kings 9; 2 Chronicles 8 Proverbs 25-26	Proverbs 27-29 Ecclesiastes 1-6 Ecclesiastes 7-12 1 Kings 10-11; 2 Chronicles 9 Proverbs 30-31 1 Kings 12-14 2 Chronicles 10-12

1 Kings 15:1-24; 2 Chronicles 13-16 1 Kings 15:25-16:34; 2 Chronicles 17 1 Kings 17-19 1 Kings 20-21 1 Kings 22; 2 Chronicles 18 2 Chronicles 19-23 Obadiah; Psalms 82-83	2 Kings 1-4 2 Kings 5-8 2 Kings 9-11 2 Kings 12-13; 2 Chronicles 24 2 Kings 14; 2 Chronicles 25 Jonah 2 Kings 15; 2 Chronicles 26	Isaiah 1-4 Isaiah 5-8 Amos 1-5 Amos 6-9 2 Chronicles 27; Isaiah 9-12 Micah 2 Chronicles 28; 2 Kings 16-17	Isaiah 13-17 Isaiah 18-22 Isaiah 23-27 2 Kings 18:1-8; 2 Chronicles 29-31; Psalms 48 Hosea 1-7 Hosea 8-14 Isaiah 28-30	Isaiah 31-34 Isaiah 35-36 Isaiah 37-39; Psalms 76 Isaiah 40-43 Isaiah 44-48 2 Kings 18:9-19:37; Psalms 46, 80, 135 Isaiah 49-53

Isaiah 54-58 Isaiah 59-63 Isaiah 64-66 2 Kings 20-21 2 Chronicles 32-33 Nahum 2 Kings 22-23; 2 Chronicles 34-35	Zephaniah Jeremiah 1-3 Jeremiah 4-6 Jeremiah 7-9 Jeremiah 10-13 Jeremiah 14-17 Jeremiah 18-22	Jeremiah 23-25 Jeremiah 26-29 Jeremiah 30-31 Jeremiah 32-34 Jeremiah 35-37 Jeremiah 38-40; Psalms 74, 79 2 Kings 24-25; 2 Chronicles 36	Habakkuk Jeremiah 41-45 Jeremiah 46-48 Jeremiah 49-50 Jeremiah 51-52 Lamentations 1:1-3:36 Lamentations 3:37-5:22	Ezekiel 1-4 Ezekiel 5-8 Ezekiel 9-12 Ezekiel 13-15 Ezekiel 16-17 Ezekiel 18-19 Ezekiel 20-21

Ezekiel 22-23 Ezekiel 24-27 Ezekiel 28-31 Ezekiel 32-34 Ezekiel 35-37 Ezekiel 38-39 Ezekiel 40-41	Ezekiel 42-43 Ezekiel 44-45 Ezekiel 46-48 Joel Daniel 1-3 Daniel 4-6 Daniel 7-9	Daniel 10-12 Ezra 1-3 Ezra 4-6; Psalms 137 Haggai Zechariah 1-7 Zechariah 8-14	Esther 1-5 Esther 6-10 Ezra 7-10 Nehemiah 1-5 Lamentations 3:37-5:22 Nehemiah 6-7 Nehemiah 11-13 Matthew 1	Psalms 126 Malachi Luke 1- 2:1-38 John 1:1-14 Matthew 2; Luke 2:39-52 Matthew 3; Mark 1; Luke 3 Matthew 4; Luke 4-5; John 1:15-51 John 2-4

Matthew 8-9; Mark 2 John 5 Matthew 12:1-21; Mark 3; Luke 6 Matthew 5-7 Matthew 8:1-13; Luke 7 Matthew 11 Matthew 12:22-50; Luke 11	Matthew 13; Luke 8 Matthew 8:14-34; Mark 4-5 Matthew 9-10 Matthew 14; Mark 6; Luke 9:1-17 John 6 Matthew 15; Mark 7 Matthew 16; Mark 8; Luke 9:18-27 Matthew 17; Mark 9; John 7-8	Luke 9:28-62 Matthew 18 John 9:1-10:21 Luke 10-11; John 10:22-42 Luke 12-13 Luke 14-15 Luke 16-17:10 John 11	Luke 17:11-18:14 Matthew 19; Mark 10 Matthew 20-21 Luke 18:15-19:48 Mark 11; John 12 Matthew 22; Mark 12 Matthew 23; Luke 20-21	Mark 13 Matthew 24 Matthew 25 Matthew 26; Mark 14 Luke 22; John 13 John 14-17 Matthew 27; Mark 15

Luke 23; John 18-19 Matthew 28; Mark 16 Luke 24; John 20-21 Acts 1-3 Acts 4-6 Acts 7-8 Acts 9-10	Acts 11-12 Acts 13-14 James Acts 15-16 Galatians 1-3 Galatians 4-6 Acts 17-18:18	1 Thessalonians; 2 Thessalonians Acts 18:19-19:41 1 Corinthians 1-4 1 Corinthians 5-8 1 Corinthians 9-11 1 Corinthians 12-14 1 Corinthians 15-16	2 Corinthians 1-4 2 Corinthians 5-9 2 Corinthians 10-13 Acts 20:1-3; Romans 1-3 Romans 4-7 Romans 8-10 Romans 11-13	Romans 14-16 Acts 20:4-23:35 Acts 24-26 Acts 27-28 Colossians; Philemon Ephesians Philippians

1 Timothy Titus 1 Peter Hebrews 1-6 Hebrews 7-10 Hebrews 11-13 2 Timothy	2 Peter; Jude 1 John 2 John; 3 John Dates Covered: 8 B.C. - A.D. 96. Secular Events: 1. Mount Vesuvius Erupts A.D. 79. 2. Claudius conquers Britain for Rome A.D. 43. 3. Construction begins on Roman Coliseum A.D. 71. Revelation 1-5 Revelation 6-11 Revelation 12-18 Revelation 19-22

What did writing The Bible Summary for REAL People mean to and for me?

Why would anyone intentionally write a summary of the Bible for REAL people? No one really would, but in the end, I really wanted to write this book because so many of my radio and podcast listeners were asking for a simple, easy to understand, concise summary of each book of the Bible.

This book is as a direct result of a course required of every first year undergrad student at Master's School of Divinity, Evansville, Indiana (Now Master's International School of Divinity www.Mdivs.edu). You cannot move forward at Master's without successfully completing this undergraduate course. The name of the course is aptly named "Bible Mastery."

This is how reading the Bible with specific purpose of writing this commentary/summaryimpacted my understanding of the Bible. This is how it helped me in the application of the Bible to my personal life; and how this understanding has changed the way I think and react in matters related to the Bible as a whole.

In the course of completing this original project I found myself starting and restarting the course work because I wasn'tconfident the end result was the best product I could produce. Though I am typically a meticulous guy, I am certain my reticence to complete the course was the restraining issue. The obstacle was not in the sheer volume of words to be written, because as anyone who has read my academic undergraduate, graduate, and post graduate work would assert, a shortage of opinion and words is not my problem, though those same folks and professorsmight say it probably should be!

The obstacle might seem at first to be the eighty hour work weeks spent running my company, preaching, writing for other projects, raising my family, and trying to stay physically alive. I came to the conclusion that could not be the case because I read three to four books per month, study the Bible one to three hours a day, and have time to write sermons and counsel folks.

Through much prayer and wise counsel I realized the primary obstacle in timely completion of the Bible Mastery Course which birthed this book was the awe I feel for this amazing book written by so many, inspired by only One. In the process of culling my thoughts on each book of this Bible I found myself writing synopses of each book, reading the synopsis and finding that though accurate, it has been written many times by other more capable authors than I.

My honest struggle was in the realization that I should be annotating **what each book means to me,** within the bounds of accurate exposition of the book of the Bible.

Upon that realization it seemed to open an entirely different discussion between my mind and heart. This discussion centered on the intense disgust I had for my suboptimal level of knowledge of this book after so many years of "studying" it.

I had to ask myself the hard questions about why I didn't have more of the Bible memorized when I actually had a memory?

A fatal 92mph vs 51mph head on car crash several years ago erased the memorized portions of my brain for the most part, but what of my time since? Why hadn't I been able to state chapter and verse, as I had been able to do before? The conclusion came to me during study one night; **I simply was trying too hard.**

My dear professor and friend, Dr. Ronald Frazier, in his wise counsel, told me much the same thing. After my real and raw conversation with Dr. Frazier and my dear friend and Professor, founding President of my Divinity School, Master's International School of Divinity, Dr. Frey, then my process became freer and much more fulfilling.

These are two great MEN of God who sowed into my life as no other ever has.

Not that I ever felt a sense of toil or dread in reading the Bible, I love this Book and all that it stands for. Rather, I simply began to trust God for discernment on a heart level and following was some of the most uplifting Bible study I have ever had. I leaned into wind of the breathing Word of the King.

I cannot tell you accurately what Master's Divinity School means to me because it is simply so large a description that might well belie words. I can tell you that in every course and the aftermath of it, my mind and faith have been shaped by the mandate to "cut God's Word straight." To "Cut it straight" one must study deeply the Words of the pages, the precepts of the Author, and the rebuking by the Master.

The Master's Divinity School undergraduate course, *Bible Mastery* is likely intimidating to many students for many other reasons than I have cited. Having written a 129-pagedoctoral dissertation the scope of the project was not intimidating to me.

What was trepid was the fact that once again I would have to confront the humbling Words of the Master and again be removed from the realm of plausible deniability. I read the Words, cover-to-cover, tear and blood stained pages of Christ woven through every page. Once I knew the Truth I cannot any longer make the claim I know not the Truth. Soli Deo Gloria!

Thank you for reading my work. I truly hope as you've read my book about THE Book, that you experienced Scripture fully and deeply. That was and is my goal!

Today is a great day to be ALIVE!

Here is how you can follow my other work:

www.DrShawnGreener.com - When you visit, **Subscribe!**
https://www.facebook.com/smgreener - Click on **Follow!**
https://www.instagram.com/theninjapastor/ - Click on **Follow!**
https://twitter.com/theninjapastor - Click on **Follow!**

To listen and Subscribe to my weekly radio show:
Sundays, 5:30pm Eastern.

For Desktop
https://www.spreaker.com/show/the-ninja-pastor-radio-show

You can both listen and follow at the above Spreaker App OR!!!!

You can download our own Radio Show Smartphone APP!!! FREEEEE!!!!

Android App
https://play.google.com/store/apps/details…

iPhone App
https://itunes.apple.com/…/the-ninja-pastor-r…/id1283330145…

To follow my photography and to purchase my art please see:

The Innovative Photography of Dr. Shawn Greener

https://shawnm-greener.pixels.com/ - While you are there, SUʙ.c.IBE!

Observing and Creating Compelling images, which slow a rushed mind, uplift a down spirit, and inspire toward better moments and memories… Shawn's Signature Concierge Photography presents moments that may only happen once in a lifetime… Images of timely and timeless relevance.

Thank you so much for connecting with me and I would appreciate your comments and feedback! God bless you!

www.StillLivingPhotography.com

All the best,
Shawn
Reverend Dr. Shawn Michael Greener
"The Ninja Pastor®
smgreener@gmail.com

CPSIA information can be obtained
at www.ICGtesting.com
Printed in the USA
LVHW110950070921
697203LV00006B/24

9 781951 469573